Cry and You Cry Alone

Rosalinda V. Hutton has worked as a legal secretary and as an English lecturer. She has an honours degree in humanities and currently works with adults with learning difficulties and mental-health problems.

Cry and You Cry Alone

The Girl Who Vowed She'd Never Forget

Rosalinda V. Hutton

MAINSTREAM
PUBLISHING

EDINBURGH AND LONDON

First published in Great Britain in 2011 by
MAINSTREAM PUBLISHING COMPANY
(EDINBURGH) LTD
7 Albany Street
Edinburgh EH1 3UG

ISBN 9781845967659

This book is a work of non-fiction based on the life, experiences and recollections of the
author. In some cases, names of people have been changed to protect the privacy of
others. The author has stated to the publishers that, except in such respects not affecting
the substantial accuracy of the work, the contents of this book are true.

All picture section images courtesy of the author

A catalogue record for this book is available
from the British Library

Printed in Great Britain by
Clays Ltd St Ives plc

1 3 5 7 9 10 8 6 4 2

Acknowledgements

....

I would like to dedicate this book to the memory of my beloved dad, Frank (Francis) Harris Hutton, whose constant love, support, laughter and guidance enabled me to pick myself up, dust myself down and face the world with confidence. A wonderful dad and a wonderful grandad, his strength of character, compassion, wisdom, laughter and *savoir faire* were the rock on which we, his descendants, base our lives. My dad always knew that I would write this book. I think he knew, too, that I would not do it in his lifetime, though we never spoke about it. I have his written 'go ahead' in the last birthday card I ever received from him.

I would also like to dedicate this book to the memory of my beloved mother, who was as she was, a big character with a mischievous twinkle in her eye and a giggle constantly bubbling beneath the surface. I thank her for giving me her blessing to write this book and I will always regret the years I spent apart from her.

I would like to thank all my wonderful friends, Big Lynn and Chris especially, Chris for all her help with this book and Chris's mum, Pat, and sisters, Caroline and Vicky, for always making me feel like part of the family. Thank you, too, to Samantha, Jak's 'Mamf', for being the lovely daughter I never had. My love and thanks to Rita for her strength and support throughout the trial and after.

Thank you to Neil Nixon, Pauline Hall and Mike Ellis, my former lecturers, for opening the doors to education and making it so interesting and exciting, and thank you to Sue, who shared the journey, Sam, Steve, Michaela, Paul, Nina and our great class of '99.

I want to thank my colleagues and friends. Thanks to Ken Hazel for being such a brilliant boss who understands his staff and his clients and is adored by all. Thank you, Frances, for teaching me that wonderful pearl of wisdom 'she is as she is' and thank you to all the lovely staff at LR, especially Lydia, Janice and Sania.

Thank you also to David Greenwood of Jordans Solicitors for believing in me and believing in the case enough to take it on, and to Joanna Beazley Richards for her caring and sensitive approach to my case and for the amazing work that she does with the survivors of historic child abuse. Thank you to Bill Campbell for taking a chance on me, and to all at Mainstream, including Graeme, Karyn, Claire and Fiona.

And finally I would also like to dedicate this book to my two sons, Terry and Jak, who have grown up to be all I ever dreamed of and more.

❉   ❉   ❉

Laugh, and the world laughs with you;
   Weep, and you weep alone;
For the sad old earth must borrow its mirth,
   But has trouble enough of its own.

'Solitude', Ella Wheeler Wilcox

Contents

Preface

The Journey of a Lifetime

In May 2010, I attended the trial of my claim against the Trustees of the Institute of Our Lady of Mercy and the local Catholic Children's Society for the abuse I had suffered as a child in an orphanage at St Anne's Convent in Orpington, Kent, from 1968 until 1972. At the age of ten, I had been found living alone in a one-bedroom bedsit in Whitton and was taken into care by the London Borough of Richmond before being passed over to the care of the Catholic Church and the Sisters of Mercy, who ran the orphanage. In court, the defendants claimed that any psychological damage I had incurred was as a result of my traumatic childhood prior to being rescued.

Very few people undergo the ordeal of being psychologically dissected by experts on opposite sides, or stand accused of being a bad person from a bad family, accused of being a liar, or a fantasist, or a chancer trying to steal a wodge of cash from the gentle and merciful women of God. It is amazing how much you come to appreciate your loved ones when you are put in the position of defending them. In the witness box, I became not the claimant but the defendant, the accused – and the prize became my sanity.

The trial became a huge battle within my mind as I fought to remember the bold little girl I used to be and understand what I had become. As an adult, I'd lost the confidence I'd once had. I wasn't sure who I was any more. According to my psychologist, I had disassociated, my personality had split; I had created other 'selves', some that I was not even aware of. I knew the bold little girl was still inside me somewhere: she was the one who got me into trouble, the one whose behaviour was inappropriate, embarrassing even, but she was also the one who laughed, the one who wasn't afraid of anything. I needed her now I was about to relive, in graphic detail, the horrors I had endured while in the care of the Sisters of Mercy and an insane former Jesuit monk.

I knew in many ways that the truth and even the evidence might be of little consequence because the verdict could rest on the limitation argument. In cases of historic child abuse, the verdict can depend on the timescales given in the statute of limitations: that is, the time in which to bring a claim. Most claims are beyond the acceptable timescale according to the letter of the law, but some are successful at trial and some are not. Mine was more than 35 years old. It is a grey area of the law that basically boils down to the individual judge's discretion.

Mine was expected to become a landmark case, one that would go into the statute books as part of an 'Idiot's Guide' to historic abuse cases for judges and members of the judiciary. A ruling the wrong way had the potential to put another few nails in the coffin of any future claims in the UK. In Ireland, the Catholic Church has accepted liability for the abuse that took place in their care homes and the claimants are now spared the ordeal of a trial. In England, the Catholic Church fights each claim with a vengeance.

I should note here that there were in fact two defence barristers, one for each of the Catholic Church organisations. One of these barristers took a more aggressive line of questioning than the other and as such made more of an impression on me. I have therefore included parts of his cross-examination alone in the account that follows.

The whole case became a David and Goliath battle. My chances became slimmer by the day and the trial became a dark, grotesque torture of the mind that I could never have imagined. My barrister and solicitor put our chances of winning at 50–50. This is my story.

Day One

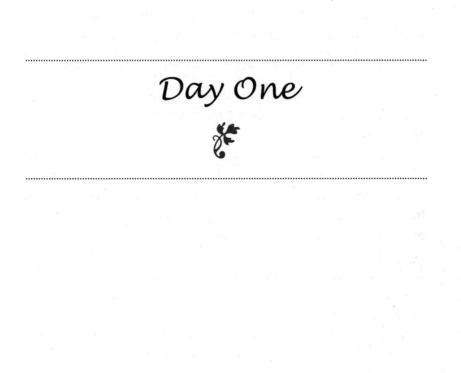

Chapter 1
The Trial Begins:
A Claimant Such as You

'In all my years at the bar, I have never heard a claimant use the word "malevolent" – did you write that, or did your solicitor?'

I stood in the witness box and looked at the barrister as he rocked back and forth on his heels, his arms folded and his head strategically held back so he could look down the line of his nose as he spoke to me.

I stared around the courtroom: it was full, and it was one of the larger courtrooms, too. Were they really all here to listen to little old me? I had watched earlier as they wheeled in boxes and boxes of files, followed by barristers in their wigs and gowns, closely shadowed by their clerks and the solicitors and their clerks, pens and notepads at the ready to record every word uttered. I had been in a courtroom before – just the previous year, actually. I had been called as a juror in a knife-crime trial and I had watched the proceedings as an outsider, detached and neutral, saddened by the details of the case but bemused and fascinated by the archaic setting and the pomp and ceremony. I had stifled a giggle when the judge repeated the witness's words for those who hadn't heard: he said 'fuck orf, you barstard' as only a judge can. Of course, I kept my head down. I knew if I had caught the eye of anyone else who was laughing, that would have been it. I have always been a giggler.

But I wasn't detached from this: this was my life, and they were all staring up at me, pens at the ready, waiting for my reply. I felt my eyes blur, not with tears but with a kind of semi-blindness: all I could see were the hazy faces of those in the front row and the blinding whiteness of m'lud's white bib. Then I heard a lucid, clear, confident voice, though somehow I couldn't understand what it was saying. Evidently one of my multiple personalities had come to my rescue. Inwardly I had scorned the advice of my expert psychologist: multiple personalities indeed! The idea was preposterous. I had gone along with it, of course; she was such a nice lady, and I didn't want to harm my case. Besides, I had just spent eight hours undergoing tests that even Martians would struggle to come up with, and by the time I had been mentally prodded and probed in every conceivable position I didn't know who the fuck I was.

Was I the bold little Irish girl again in that courtroom, the misfit, the pauper, with 'how dare you?' ringing in my ears? How often I had heard those words.

'I can't remember,' I replied, as I struggled to find an answer to the barrister's question.

'Isn't "malevolent" the most descriptive word?' The judge had come to my assistance.

Yes, it was the most descriptive word, and maybe it was mine, maybe not, but surely it was just a word, like any other? I had used the word in my written statement to describe the spiteful behaviour of the 'uncle' who had been in charge of me at St Anne's Convent, and Omni, as I called the barrister, had picked up on it. He could not understand how a person like me, a mere claimant, probably dragged from the holding pen of *The Jeremy Kyle Show*, could know such a word.

His intention was to belittle me, to remind me who I was. 'Was it your word or was it your solicitor's?' Again, he pressed me for an answer. He was trying to show the court that I had been coached, that someone much cleverer than me had put the statement together. Or was he just trying to humiliate me? Either way, he had me stumped. I could not think of an answer. Well, not one that would leave me with any credibility. I wanted to scream out at him, 'I got educated, you bastard! I know that word – I've got a degree!' I was fuming. In an instant, Omni had hit my Achilles heel. I had worked so hard to pull myself up from the gutter. I hated my past; I had kept it hidden, even from myself. I wasn't that person! I have always worked, I have impeccable good manners, I read books, I can discuss Voltaire or Picasso and I make the best roast dinner in the world, but I still wasn't good enough. I physically shrank as my confidence ebbed away. My greatest achievement has been my two sons, who have grown up to be everything I ever hoped for and more; I would be so ashamed if they could see him talking to me this way. My heart was breaking. Here in this courtroom, it was all a sham. I was the street rat again.

I had no answer for Omni. Nothing I could say would get me out of this stalemate, and I knew that I wouldn't be able to hide my anger. I cursed my stupidity. I had read enough books and seen enough courtroom dramas to know that this is the game barristers play. They know which buttons to press, which nerves are exposed. One could even say their knowledge justified their exorbitant salaries. They are experts in all human behaviour, except their own.

Omni had me on the ropes, and we were only about ten minutes into the trial. So much for the impeccable fantasy performance that I had envisaged so many times in my head.

It was Day One and I had been sworn in as the first witness to give evidence in my case against the two Catholic Church organisations, which, apparently, had had a duty to protect me when I was a child. The usher had given me the option of several cards to read out loud to the entire court, depending on my religious affiliations. I would like to say I gave it a great deal of thought at the time, but I didn't, I just screwed my eyes up and tried to spot which one was the agnostic, atheist or even Buddhist one. I quite like Buddhism and I could kick myself for not asking for a Buddhist version, just for the hell of it. I chose the atheist one but could feel the presence of my dead Irish grandmother, waving her fist and yelling, 'Ya heathen!' It made me smile.

'So let's get back to the hovel you were found in. Please turn to page 248 of your social worker's file,' the barrister said. I knew he had used the word 'hovel' to cause maximum hurt, and it did, it had the desired effect. Wow, he was good! He might just as well have said, 'Who do you think you are? Remember where you came from, missy.' He was a caricature, a cruel, thin-lipped Dickensian baddie from some parallel universe, a time-warp tunnel with a direct link to the nineteenth century. He had compared the cruel, brutal regime of St Anne's Convent to the jolly japes of a public-school dorm, and the judge had laughed and agreed. Well, he would, wouldn't he?

The usher handed me the large ring binder of papers and grumpily pretended to assist me in locating the page. He kept his head bowed always; he didn't dare look me in the eye. It was as if he could barely hide his contempt.

And there it was, written on faded old documents in front of me. Every excruciating detail set out in black and white, accompanied by a whoosh of paper shuffling as each participant in this bizarre Greek tragedy turned their pages in unison.

I gazed down at the words before me. It was like *This Is Your Life* with added torture. It was hard to concentrate on the barrister's words as I read descriptions of my young parents and the poverty that our family had been reduced to.

Chapter 2
Meet Big Lynn

The night before, Big Lynn had sat next to me on the coach and squeezed my hand, letting me know everything would be OK, as we travelled up to Leeds from London. Her upbeat mood and sense of reality kept me grounded. She had always promised me she would accompany me to this trial. And she did.

Big Lynn and I met in our first jobs, aged 15, just after I had left the convent, and we had become lifelong pals. We were the Laurel and Hardy of friends, with me at 5 ft 2 in. and Lynn over 6 ft tall. She was a great big cockney bird, loud, brash, very accident-prone and fiercely proud of her working-class roots. Big Lynn would always storm in and take charge of every crisis, and having her by my side was like having a guardian angel on my shoulder. Instinctively she picked up on my every mood swing, my every panic, and steered me back to my happy place. As eccentric as I am, she always had the ability to see the absurd in every situation and we would always end up laughing. Even though I was seemingly facing the hanging judge with his gavel, Lynn and I agreed that the architecture of the court building was nice, but they could do with some new curtains.

I knew Lynn wouldn't let me down over her lifelong promise to accompany me to the trial, but when I drove over to see her the day before we were due to travel up to Leeds for it, I almost hoped she would. We had been speaking on the phone and she told me that she had had an 'accident with a lawnmower' and had stitches in her head. I was used to Lynn having accidents – she was a clumsy moo – and though I am ashamed to admit it now, I did not take her latest mishap as seriously as I should have. She had, of course, told me that she had been taken to hospital and that they had kept her in, in case of concussion, but I was totally unprepared for how bad her injury looked. Almost the entire top right-hand side of her head had been shaved and she had a big circular wound highlighted in black stitches. I took one look at her and thought, 'We're doomed.' Potentially my one and only witness, she looked as though she had had a lobotomy!

I spent most of the night before our journey to Leeds tossing and turning, trying to think of ways to persuade her to cover the blooming thing up. I had a drawer full of scarves: perhaps I could persuade her to go with the 'hippy chick' look? It was the only option I could think of, but I couldn't insult her that way; I loved her way too much. In the end, I thought, 'Feck 'em. Big Lynn is Big Lynn, and she is worth a hundred of them lot.'

We had travelled up to Leeds on a Megabus – a cheaper version of National Express and a great bargain to paupers such as ourselves. Every minute was a hoot, spotting all the places we used to go to or used to know as the coach made its way through the myriad of London streets, property prices dwindling as we got further and further from the exclusive West End. I pointed out famous sites such as Sherlock Holmes's house, and Big Lynn pointed out the great hot-dog stands and places where we had both thrown up following drunken nights and dodgy kebabs. We tucked into an assortment of sandwiches and sweets, deciding we would deprive ourselves of nothing we fancied, bar alcohol. On a good night, we could both knock 'em back till all hours, but we knew, without saying it out loud, that this trial would be a solemn occasion and we needed to keep totally clear heads. We had waited for it for so long.

The Megabus dropped us off in the middle of Leeds at 10.30 p.m. Naturally, neither of us had had the sense to book anywhere to stay, so there we were, stranded and pretty much lost. I once heard the expression 'God looks after drunks and fallen women' and it has always stuck with me, so I was pretty sure Lynn and I would be OK. Actually, neither of us was unduly worried – perhaps panic is a man thing. Happily, a kindly local man on a bicycle stopped, asked if we were lost and then helpfully pointed out a massive semi-circular concrete mass that took up the entire south side of a bloody big roundabout that was right in front of us. Neither of us was in the least bit surprised by this act of kindness in a massive city, because we had heard about how friendly it was 'oop North' and sort of half expected it. We were quite sure the cyclist wouldn't have been after our bods and laughed at the thought of it.

The hotel in front of us was a huge, impersonal building that looked posh on the outside (we thought we wouldn't be able to afford it) but was plastic, like a smoothed-out Lego set, on the inside. We both hated it immediately, but it was cheap and it was too late to find anywhere else and our feet were killing us.

There were warning signs everywhere – 'Do Not Smoke', 'Smoking Strictly Prohibited', 'We Will Catch You If You Smoke, We Have a Pack of Rabid Rottweilers Patrolling the Corridors Who Will Rip Your Throat Out Before You Have Your Second Drag'. We decided to smoke out of the window, but the owners had put a bar there so it would only open about six inches, and there was even a smoke alarm in the shower, so they pretty much had you covered. We considered putting socks over the smoke alarms, but I think we found a sign saying we would be exterminated if we tried that one.

As we headed down to the lobby and outside to have our last dozen chain-smoked fags, I overheard someone booking a smoking room! The sheer joy of this discovery sent the pair of us into overdrive. We did not like the room, we said.

'Er, they're all exactly the same,' said the clerk at the desk.

'They've got a smoking room and we haven't,' said Big Lynn, never one to beat about the bush. Happily, the clerk took pity and agreed to transfer us.

And indeed the rooms were all exactly the same: the smallest shower/toilet built into the walls so you would hardly notice it and a double bed with a single bunk hovering overhead. 'Don't worry,' said Lynn, 'I'll climb up there.' The thought of the accident-prone Big Lynn sleeping directly above my head led me to attempt the wooden ladder, but I only got as far as the second rung before I told her to shove over in the double.

As we lay on our bed talking, it all seemed quite bizarre, even funny. I am not sure if our laughter was born of nerves or fear of what the next day held, but in each other's company we were 16 again, and unafraid. Even those deepest, darkest fears, the ones that wake you up in the early hours in a cold sweat, seemed trivial and unimportant. We had both endured tragedy throughout our lives and we had both recently lost our mothers. We were sad, but in a way we were relieved that the trial had finally arrived and would be over soon. It seemed as though we were both now free to do whatever we wanted, and we made plans for the future. We talked about driving across Europe in an open-top car, à la Thelma and Louise, but talks broke down when Lynn insisted we should live within our budget and stay in cheap B&Bs or a tent and I wanted the Ritz. As so often in our long years of friendship, we couldn't blooming agree!

Back in court on Day One, it took several moments for me to regain my composure in the witness box as Omni began to assault me with questions. I tried to make out Big Lynn at the back of courtroom. She had wanted to bring in crisps and a can of Diet Coke, but I'd strictly forbidden her. She chomped on Walkers cheese and onion crisps like a horse, getting every last crunch out of every last mouthful. 'Why don't you just get popcorn?' I teased her. I knew I could rely on her to be the most enthusiastic and vociferous member of what was meant to be a silent audience, and try as she might she couldn't keep back the 'ooh's and 'ah's and the ''ere, that's not right' indignant comments, despite all the stern looks she was getting from the judge. A couple of times I wanted to smile at her, but I didn't dare.

Lynn nicknamed the opposing barrister on the first day: 'Omni', she called him, as in omnipotent, omnipresent or 'sumfing like that', she told me as she hooted with laughter. I was, of course, a trembling wreck, surviving on beta blockers, fags and coffee. My lovely aul Big Lynn catered for my every need, fussing around me like a mother hen and averting all disasters, such as running out of fags. When I was down to my last five during a fag break, I asked her to get me some Embassy, in memory of my mother, who smoked them, rather than cheap old Mayfair. If I smoked her fags, maybe Mum would be there with me. Lynn would dutifully run off to the shop during any breaks in proceedings and only complained when I asked for the Embassy. ''Ere, do you know how much they fucking cost?' she screeched on her return, making me roar with laughter.

At the courthouse, each party was allocated a small room in which to meet and talk at the start of each day, and our team was tiny in comparison to the defendants': just my solicitor, barrister, psychologist Joanna and myself. Lynn had to wait outside, but she plonked herself next to the coffee machine and tried to earwig what the other side were saying.

Day One of the trial was the first time I had seen Joanna since the day I had spent with her undergoing all sorts of tests and experiments designed to gauge exactly how nutty I was. Joanna believed that my lifelong depression had been triggered by the trauma of the events that had occurred at St Anne's Convent. I had developed alternative personalities and would apparently physically transform as each new character took over the helm. I wasn't aware of it happening and it freaked me out. I didn't want to know and wished I was an ostrich so I could bury my head in the sand. Joanna had said that without years of therapy (which I wouldn't attend) I would never recover, never sustain long-term employment, never have a relationship.

Joanna seemed friendlier now and more forthcoming. 'You still have no idea of the damage that was done,' she said to me kindly. 'Thank goodness you had such a wonderful father.' I was glad that she'd said that about my dad. I had felt a little unnerved in her presence, as though she could see into my very soul; her psychological examination had scrutinised my every cell, as though I were undergoing a living autopsy on my brain.

Yet she didn't treat me as a case study, or at least I didn't really feel as though she did because she was genuinely warm and sympathetic. However, she had an air of professionalism about her that made our contact outside of the courtroom awkward and stilted. I longed for her to speak to me as a human being, as an equal. I knew there had to be that patient/doctor divide, of course, but the court experience had reduced me to a blubbering wreck. In that room, I was surrounded by grey and black officialdom, complete with a judge wearing everything bar a black cap to sit atop his wig when he pronounced the inevitable death sentence. My mood was low and I felt intimidated by the court and the surroundings. I didn't feel like a witness; I felt like a scoundrel in the dock, up in front of the beak for criticising the Establishment with the mob outside baying for my blood.

As I stood in the witness box, the usher placed a box file of papers in front of me, and Omni was referring me to pages and incidents. The words on the copious papers in front of me had been written by my childhood social worker, Miss Bradshaw. My brother, Colin, and I had been taken into care and appointed a small, stern but endearing elderly spinster as our social worker. I remembered her so well. They kept referring to her as Mrs Bradshaw, and that irritated me, because she wasn't a Mrs, she was a Miss and quite proud of it! She had been in our lives for several years and I think Colin and I both grew to love her. It had got off to a rocky start, for sure. We were curious when we first met her. She didn't seem to be half as clever as us, and we giggled as we thought up ways to wind her around our little fingers. It was easy-peasy, or so we thought.

She was a tiny lady with grey hair cut into a severe bob and a crocheted beret tilted to one side. She had a strong, determined face that always looked as though it had been freshly scrubbed and was devoid of any make-up. She wore belted tweed suits with a smart blouse and matching brogues, like a small and frail Miss Marple with twice the attitude. I told her I liked her berets. She made them herself, she told me, and she liked that I liked them; it made her happy. I didn't like them really: it was the swinging '60s, and hot pants and miniskirts ruled. Miss Bradshaw would visit us regularly and take us for good, hearty walks deep into the countryside. She would point out the beauty of the bluebells, or whatever flowers were coming into bloom, while Colin and I would climb as high as we could up into the trees and swing by our legs to frighten the bejesus out of her. Nothing we did made her flinch, and eventually we stopped trying and just listened to the sheer joy in her voice as she spoke of her love of musical theatre, the arts and the great outdoors.

And all her words were there in the files before me now, as I stood in the witness box. Her notes showed her to have been conscientious and dedicated to her job, going above and beyond, as I knew she would have: all that was probably expected of her back in those days. The notes were full and detailed, with enough information to give a complete picture of our lives. They were without malice and almost respectful. 'Colin and Linda's father is a small, good-humoured, well-mannered, dependable Scotsman,' they read, 'but we believe their Irish mother may have a personality disorder.' It sounded about right, I suppose, but I wished that they had put 'good-looking', because they both were. I don't know why that mattered, but it did.

I could feel the tears rising in my eyes as I looked at the volumes of ancient letters and reports in front of me. I hadn't expected this. I looked at the names, I looked at the dates, I looked at the cold, impersonal words. Those were my parents, those kids were me and my brother. It was unbelievably callous. I wondered if it was legal. It definitely wasn't moral. Did anyone, anywhere, at any time, consider the possible consequences of presenting a manic depressive with a complete and annotated file of their worst nightmares? It was a cruelty I could not have imagined. I looked towards my solicitor. He looked away. Why hadn't he told me this would happen? Both psychologists had their heads down; only Lynn looked towards me. I could see the pain on her face; she understood what I was going through.

I knew the barrister was waiting for me to find the right page and answer his question. I was shaking as I turned the pages. I was so shocked, almost reeling, as if I had received a huge blow to my body. How could such an innocuous question hurt to the very core?

'You were described as happy children,' he repeated. 'Do you not see that this contradicts your case?'

Of course I could see that, but the words related to our arrival at the convent. By the time of our departure four years later, we were different people entirely. He was twisting things deliberately, trying to get me confused.

The file contained copies of original letters and reports, some dating back to 1968. They had been typed on ancient typewriters, and some of the words were faded or had disappeared altogether. They were documents from a genteel bygone age when everything was right and proper, a time when people stood up for the Queen in the cinema while they played the national anthem. It would be just after the film had finished and you were dying to talk about it and the grown-ups behind or in front of you would put their fingers to their lips and tell you to shush. My mum never stood up for the Queen; she wouldn't even stay by her seat while the miserable old song was played. 'What do I want to stand up for that aul bitch for?' she would say to me and Colin as she rushed us out before anyone else. People used to tut and look at us disapprovingly as we ran up the aisle after her, but she just used to tell them to 'feck off'. We never used to get away any quicker, though, because Dad would always stay behind and be respectful and we would have to wait outside for him.

The papers in front of me rekindled so many memories, both good and bad. I needed to defend my parents, I needed the good memories, the positive memories, to keep my voice from trembling and my mind focused. I wasn't going to collapse or be reduced to a stuttering eejit. I was going to speak my truth, quietly and clearly. I had a gift for language, an answer for everything. I was not going to

24

allow Omni to break my spirit. I had read about previous claimants in cases such as mine who had left the witness box and gone on to commit suicide. I knew how high the stakes were, but my determination only increased.

I had vowed so many years ago never to be powerless again. Omni didn't scare me with his Batman cape and his dodgy wig, no matter how much he strutted and preened. The judge scared me a little bit: he could go from being a kindly Santa in his red coat and, frankly, much more upmarket wig than Omni's to Hanging Judge Jeffreys in an instant, banging his gavel and angrily scattering his papers around, looking for his black cap.

As I read the files in front of me, they didn't feel right. My parents weren't the one-dimensional characters that these curt, formal notes portrayed. 'It wasn't like that at all,' I wanted to scream at the barrister. I was not prepared for the evidence that had been put before me. As I stood in the witness box feeling very small and vulnerable, I glanced up and around the courtroom. All eyes were looking at me. 'You have been caught,' they accused. 'The records show you were a bright and happy-go-lucky child; it says it there in your social worker's notes.'

The barrister looked at me, clearly gloating. You have no case. He was leaning back with his hands on his hips and his right leg forward, in a stance that screamed 'gotcha'. He clasped his hands in victory and gave a nod to the judge à la Kenneth Williams, tongue firmly in cheek and a wink that said 'told you about 'er'.

Chapter 3

Back to Dark Places

The notes in front of me were from 1969, the age of Aquarius (or maybe it was just its dawning), which certainly hadn't reached the dark, gloomy place that was St Anne's Convent.

I remember entering St Anne's, that awful moment when my life, it seemed, suddenly turned from colour to black and white. The vibrant psychedelic sounds and colours of 1960s England were shut off with the slamming of the heavy oak convent doors.

Everything became dreary and grey. Even the nuns were black and white in their harsh, severe, starched habits that swished when they walked, with their rosary beads jangling from their leather belts like jailers' keys. Their hands and faces, too, the only bits of flesh they revealed, were white and pasty, as if they had never seen or felt the warmth of sunshine and didn't know what it was. Voices were never raised above a whisper, and there was no such thing as laughter.

The convent was huge and cold and so silent that our tiny footsteps echoed and thundered through the building, disturbing the sinister atmosphere of this cloistered monument to pain and suffering, a temple devoted to abstinence and discipline, completely devoid of any colour except for the crimson of the blood dripping from the saviour on the cross that hung over the doorway. Colin and I watched tearfully as the tiny figure of Miss Bradshaw faded away as she walked down the hill, returning alone to the real world and leaving us behind. She was dotty, but she was safe. She had watched over us for the previous few months and we had grown fond of her. Sister Bridget* then slammed the huge oak doors shut and we were imprisoned.

I didn't know then how bad it was going to be, but I sort of thought that I wouldn't be rushing home from school to watch *The Monkees* any more. I decided not to cry about that; well, not in front of them, anyway.

The barrister was right. It was absolutely true. I was a bright and happy child, or at least I had been once.

I knew what the barrister was trying to do. Any problems I did or did not have were attributable to my life prior to entering the convent. My parents were bad. They had the evidence to prove it.

I took a step back in the witness box, then looked at Omni with defiance. He had made it really personal, and I was unprepared for it. My head was 'bloody, but unbowed': the words of Henley rang in my ears. I remembered my parents well, and I remembered the convent too. I wasn't afraid of his questions. I remembered everything.

My beloved dad had always had a 'thing' about memory: he believed it was something you could train, and he would buy novelty 'how to train your memory' books and learn great big long lists, just to show how it could be done. 'Twenty-second of November 1963,' he drummed into the heads of my six-year-old self and my seven-year-old brother as we stood in front of him. 'This is the day John F. Kennedy died, and it is a moment in history. Remember it for ever,' Dad said. And we did, together with all the other iconic historic moments he taught us thereafter.

As I brought to mind the memories I was about to relive, I knew I would find the strength from somewhere, just as I had found it all those years ago as the huge oak convent doors had slammed behind us.

---

* The names of some fellow pupils, staff members and others have been changed to protect their privacy. Where this is the case, the first use of the name is followed by an asterisk.

Omni's questioning became more intense; he hit many raw nerves and severed a main artery. The questions were coming thick and fast. He wanted to know about my mother, he wanted to know about her odd behaviour, he wanted me to denounce her, to blame her for my miserable childhood. But I couldn't, because I didn't believe that any more. Maybe I had once, but not now. And his questions made me angrier as I thought of all those lost years, all those years when I had needed a mum, when I needed *my* mum. In her final years, I had found her again, and I found we were so alike: we shared exactly the same sense of humour and sense of the ridiculous, and I realised then how much I had loved her all along. And as Omni threw his vile and nasty questions at me, I remembered how she had cuddled me and how she had made me giggle. 'Toro, little bull, you're my little bull,' she sang to me as a child, and now her voice rang in my ears. He was wrong. She had loved me. My head was pounding, falling from side to side with the emotions gushing through my brain. He had me on my knees; I was reeling from each blow. The judge asked me if I wanted a break, but I didn't give up and I didn't give in. I held my dad's handkerchief tightly, but it was saturated with my tears, so I used the backs of my hands to wipe them away as they poured down my cheeks. I thought of my mother, and I thought of her words.

'Stay strong,' my mum had told me before they took us away to St Anne's. 'And don't ever let them see you cry. They always batter the weak ones,' she added. My mum was as tough as old boots and she was always proud to tell us that. Nobody could hurt her, not ever. 'And always hold your head up high.' She had been taught by nuns at home in Ireland, so she knew what they were like. 'And if they lay a finger on you or Colin, I will feckin' kill them.' I knew she really meant it, because she had an awful temper. I was never scared of anybody or anything when she was around.

I felt safe with Dad, too, but he would always deal with everything quietly and diplomatically, especially when pacifying neighbours and friends who Mum had upset. Mum would just get them by the throat.

Dad never used to swear either, and he hated it when Mum swore, so she would save it all up for while he was at work. She swore all the time; I think she enjoyed it, like a mischievous child. She even swore when she was in a happy mood and especially when she was laughing with her sisters and brothers. They always used to tell us kids to 'feck off and play', and the only way we could get to earwig in on what they were talking about was by asking if anyone wanted another Guinness or a gin and orange. I tried to join in once after listening to their gossip. 'Which fecking aul bitch that buys her drawers in the second-hand shop who everyone knows about?' I piped up, but Mum caught me with a clip round the head and told me to clear off before anyone could answer.

She only really used to gossip with her family, she never had much time for anyone else, and she only used to be polite if she wanted something. When she spoke to the neighbours or when we went in shops her voice would change, especially if she wanted groceries and didn't have any money. 'Oh dear, I seem to have forgotten my purse,' she would say. 'Let me pay you by cheque.' But she didn't have a cheque book either; she just used to say it so that the shopkeeper would think she was rich and tell her, 'That's OK, you can pay me another time.' Colin used to get annoyed when she put on her posh voice, but I liked it, and I used to copy the way she spoke, especially because it used to wind him up.

Memories of my parents came flooding back as I stood there in court, the good as well as the bad. So Miss Bradshaw considered my mother to have had a personality disorder, among other polite euphemisms used to describe her. Miss Bradshaw was very much old school, and I knew there would be nothing more graphic in her notes, though it was implied. The two women could not have been more different. Miss Bradshaw, in her comely tweeds, was the type of lady who wrote all the rules, double-checked their grammar and then followed them dutifully. Mum, with her beehive updo and minidress, was the terrible woman who broke them.

Memories of my life before the convent filled my head. I had been a happy child, I remembered how I used to be, but something had changed, and here in this stark, formal courtroom, among all these strangers in their wigs and gowns and black and white suits, my past was about to be dissected and laid bare. Joanna had told me to remember the child I had been and draw my strength from that.

Omni looked at me, his chin jutting out, daring me to speak. Behind him were many rows, perhaps eight to ten, of wooden benches, like pews in a church. They were filled with expressionless faces, rows of smart grey and black suits, legal professionals whose formal attire elevated their status above the hoi polloi whose lives they tear to shreds on a daily basis. Even Big Lynn wore black and white, but her outfit shrieked glamour; her black top shimmered with sequins against the white lace trim of her sensible cardie, and big, dangly, fake-diamond earrings drew attention to the massive great bald spot in the centre of her head. Joanna stood at the back, next to Lynn, wearing a brightly coloured trouser suit that looked all the more vivid against the luminous blonde of her platinum bun. There was nothing black, white or grey about Joanna. I wondered if her look was slightly defiant.

The witness box was positioned in a corner of the court, elevated and set apart. I felt utterly alone. The judge was sitting to the left of me, his chair and bench raised so that he could look down on the rest of us. The usher sat directly in front of the judge, standing up and sitting down, moving silently as he discreetly ensured the smooth running of the proceedings. He passed documents to the judge and jumped up to assist him with his files or with whatever His Honour desired. He was supposed to assist me, too, but he made me feel like a nuisance, and I took his expressionless face to be contemptuous. Then at the very back of the court, on the chairs against the wall, was Big Lynn, her thumbs held up in the air, and I could just make out her eyes blinking furiously, willing me on, telling me, 'You can do it, kid.'

Chapter 4
And Darker Still

Omni's questions were taking me into the worst, darkest places, those that had been safely tucked away in some hidden corner of my mind. I had expected to be questioned about the convent – I was fully prepared for that – but for some reason it hadn't occurred to me that the case would go even further back than that. It sounds so naive now.

The questioning was grotesquely cruel. Yes, I had been found alone in a hovel at the age of ten. We had lost our idyllic home in Surrey after my parents' marriage crumbled, and my father had sent me and Colin to Ireland to live with my mother's relatives. I had no idea how long we had been out there – weeks and months had just run into each other – when one day my father and mother turned up together to fetch us. We ended up in the squalid bedsit in Whitton after we returned from Ireland, but, as yet, we didn't have anywhere to live. Mum could never have accepted filling in forms for National Assistance or hanging about on a council waiting list. She hated officials and 'pen-pushers' and always wanted to get hold of them by the throat. If she wanted something, she wanted it there and then, she wanted it now. But I suspect that, even if she had behaved herself, in the early 1960s the help simply wasn't there.

At the time of the trial, I had long since forgiven my mother for our chaotic, unconventional life and accepted her for the eccentric that she was. It had only been months since she had died, and I was still grieving. I knew the circumstances I had been found in had been bad, but I needed to defend her.

Omni was looking at me, waiting for me to answer. He was tapping his foot and stroking his chin as if to say hurry up, but I couldn't tear my eyes away from the ancient documents in front of me.

'You claimed in your visit to a psychologist in 1997 that your problems were due to your mother, did you not, Miss Hutton?'

It was true: I had, because that was what I believed then. Everyone knows that if your mother doesn't love you, you are destined to be a loser. It wasn't what I meant at all. How could I explain? It was what I had believed at that time – I hadn't known any different, I hadn't asked the right questions, I hadn't researched the right texts and, more importantly, I hadn't listened to the right people. My beloved dad had never condemned my mother and she gave him a lifetime of stories and anecdotes, some desperately sad but some hilariously funny. As kids, the harshest thing he ever said about Mum was to take things she said with a pinch of salt. He knew innately how wrong it is to drive a wedge between a child and its mother. My close, lifelong friends always smoothed the path and urged me to see her, to appreciate her and love her, as she was. As we all age and grow wiser over the years, we begin to appreciate others and indulge their eccentricities, having acquired a few of our own. We now know the harsh realities of life. We have experienced pain and loss and we have all made bad decisions and suffered the consequences. Who was I to judge my mother? The idea was ridiculous. She had loved me, and that was all that really mattered. Sometimes we should just forgive and forget, because it is better to have that person in your life than not. I was having to prove to this zealous bewigged rottweiler that my mother had loved me. It was a surreal situation to be in, but I felt a perverse satisfaction. He wasn't proving the defendants' case; he was proving mine. I didn't care what he thought, or the judge or all the watchers with their pens at the ready. My mother had loved me, and I felt like leaning back and letting out a sinister cackle. Phew, tons of baggage being stripped away. And the more I thought of happy memories, the stronger I became.

Nevertheless, I had never seen those files from the 1960s before; I never knew they existed. It was painful seeing those words in front of me, and again I felt tears welling up within my eyes. I briefly looked over at Omni. He was pretending to fiddle with his papers now, hardly bothered by the delay. He had picked up on my suffering and was biding his time, and he paused to allow the pain of the words in the document to fully sink in.

Miss Bradshaw's words were clear and unequivocal. There it was in black and white: 'Colin and Linda are bright and happy children.' It was dated July 1968, before we entered the convent.

My eyes kept going back to documents in front of me, and I fixed on the words 'the mother has a personality disorder'. I suppose Mum did have a personality disorder, I thought, as I blinked back a tear, but it was so hard to see it written there. I knew even as a child, of course, that she was eccentric, that she wasn't like any other mother I had ever met, even though sometimes I really wanted her to be. I knew that she did crazy things, but she was funny and silly and giggly, and she made us giggle too. She would never let us go to sleep; she would tickle us and say daft things so we couldn't stop laughing. She did love us. I wanted to scream at Omni, 'She did love me!'

'You were sharing a pull-out sofa with your mother and brother, were you not?' Omni repeated the question again, more forcefully this time, and his question was intended to hurt, to increase my pain, to wear me down so that I would break and admit that my parents had caused my psychological damage, not the nuns and not the convent and not Peter Rands.

'Yes, we shared the sofa, but it wasn't like you said.' I tried to answer his question, but my emotions were stifling my voice and I could only manage a whisper. 'We played sleepy trains,' I said. 'We played sleepy trains.' I couldn't stop the flow of the tears running down my cheeks and I knew I sounded pathetic, but how could I tell him, how could I tell the court, how could I make them understand? 'When we were in Ireland, there were sometimes ten in a bed; it wasn't that big a deal.' I didn't care about the tears; I stuck my chin out defiantly. Omni merely sighed and looked down at his papers, carelessly writing down the words I had just spoken. I looked around the courtroom and I could see a couple of the younger female clerks smile benevolently at me, though I didn't know if it was prompted by pity or curiosity.

'So Sister Consolata called you "Madam Hutton".' Omni took his time and stood back, chewing carelessly on his pen, giving the court several moments to hear how ridiculous that sounded. 'And you think you should be compensated for that?' He was getting my mad up now, taunting me, mocking. He had changed tack and brought the questioning back to the convent years, implying that name-calling was trivial in comparison with how I had been found in Whitton.

I took my time replying, naively unprepared for this onslaught but knowing inside that I was more than ready to reply. I had lived this scene so many times in my head, not just from the beginning of this court case but for many years before, too.

I wanted desperately to reply, but I was in turmoil. I wanted it all to stop; I wanted to run away. Then my voice kicked in, but it was detached and it wasn't mine, at least I don't think it was; it was strong and it was forceful, and it quivered with emotion, and it didn't stop, and it kept speaking and speaking. That part of me that was strong had returned to the forefront, and she was unstoppable. I knew her well.

The trial wasn't about the convent; it was about my life before. Not content merely to play to win, they were out to destroy me. They wanted to soil every happy memory I had left. And in doing so, they were brushing the evidence about the convent under the carpet. There was very little there they could refute there, so they were changing the focus of the trial. I knew what Omni was doing, but it was getting to me, wearing me down. I felt exhausted, but I was angry and emotional and determined to speak out, I demanded to be heard.

'How can you defend them?' I screamed. I didn't know where this anger had come from. I had never seen it or experienced it before. It was the angriest I had ever been. Yet I had never spoken so clearly, or so passionately, in my entire life. I was finally up on my coveted soapbox, condemning the inhumanity, the cruelty, the hypocrisy. 'Do you know how it feels,' I ranted at Omni, 'to stand shivering in line, not knowing whether or not you would be hauled out of that line for an evening of their bizarre, sadistic entertainment?' In the witness box, I re-enacted the positions of the inquisitors, jabbing a pointed finger into the air to demonstrate their particular style of interrogation. The tears were cascading down my cheeks, until my voice fell to a whisper. All around me, heads were down and tears were being wiped away.

I could see Omni getting bored, looking down at his papers and turning the pages with an expression that said, 'Oh, do hurry up.' At the back of the court, I could see Lynn with her head tilted sympathetically, and I could see the sheer compassion on the face of my psychologist, Joanna. Perhaps she thought I had finally flipped.

I had seen her piles of textbooks on multiple personalities strategically placed on the chairs beside her at the back of the court, references marked with different-coloured Post-it notes, academic evidence to support her thesis. I had also seen Joanna's written report, her psychological breakdown of my inner psyche. I didn't really understand the tests or the results, other than that she thought I was an all-round good egg and not a liar.

I had tried not to let the psychological reports get to me. I was curious as hell, of course, to know the results – who wouldn't be? Joanna's report alone ran to more than 100 pages. I doubt many people have had, or would want to have, their inner selves so thoroughly dissected by expert psychologists. I experienced mood swings, of course – who doesn't? – real highs and real lows, but rarely anger. During my lows, I would shut myself away and read endlessly; it didn't really feel like a problem. I loved solitude and I loved my books. 'Why don't you go out and live life instead of reading about it?' my dad used to shout at me in exasperation. And

I did, but I felt at odds with the world, like an outsider looking in – or at least I did when I felt low. When my mood went high, my behaviour was the opposite. We all have parts of our psychological make-up that step forward to handle the difficult bits, don't we? I had all the classic signs of bipolar disorder, surely?

I didn't really mind what Miss Bradshaw had written about my mum: actually, I thought it was quite mild. Mum was enough to have made Freud hurl himself out of a top-floor window. She lived life by her own rules and bent any others that got in her way. Sometimes, even if the rules made sense, she would do the opposite, just for the hell of it. She could go from Lady Bracknell to Eliza Doolittle in the blink of an eye, and she could give you a knowing look of shared humour that could make you giggle helplessly as others looked on as if you were mad. I suppose Miss Bradshaw's summary of 'personality disorder' was correct. My mother had several different characters on the go at any one time, and I didn't have a clue which one of them Miss Bradshaw had met.

Omni was looking at me with an expression that made me feel unworthy and small, and with one nonchalant wave of his arm he dismissed all I'd said about the convent as superfluous and not relevant to the trial. He looked as though he were looking forward to his lunch at the local bistro and was trying to hurry things along, almost as though he could barely spare the time to be there. To me, it was as if he was relishing his victories and could hardly wait to regale his chums with each and every killer blow. He kept swishing his black gown, flaring it out as he stood up and pulling it back up over his shoulders to greet his stark white bib and the distinguished grey of his wise-man wig.

'"Madam Hutton" was usually followed by a punch to the face or a night of gruelling, pointless chores,' I told him boldly, but my words sounded hollow and meaningless and trivial, and I was incapable of portraying how cold and callous and terrifying that particular name-calling had once sounded. Omni's eyes were hard; he was trying to turn me into that trembling, quivering, frightened child again. I knew what he was doing, and in a way it was working.

I pulled my dad's handkerchief from out of my sleeve. My beloved dad: I thought of him as I clutched it to me. Dad always had fresh, clean, ironed handkerchiefs, never tissues. It was drenched, but I used it now to dab the tears that were flowing from my eyes. I had never been a 'crier': well, never in the convent; I wouldn't give them that satisfaction. I saw the way Sister Consolata would tease and torment any child who cried, and though I cried in front of her once, I was never going to give her that victory again. If I ever felt tears coming, I would choke them back or run and hide until they were under control.

I wasn't the prototypical victim of institutional abuse: I have no criminal record, I have worked all my life and I have gained a degree as a mature student. I had no skeletons Omni could pull out of the wardrobe to wreck my credibility. I had not labelled myself as an alcoholic or a drug abuser, nor was I mentally incompetent. Omni was finding it difficult to break me. It felt like a war of words between us. As his questions delved deeper and became more cruel and personal, my emotions took over; I was blubbing here in this courtroom, powerless, out of control. I had never lost control before, not through alcohol, or drugs, or during therapy. I had always been fully aware of exactly what I was doing and what I was saying.

Omni was taking me back in time. Like an accomplished but immoral hypnotist, he was digging up painful and traumatic memories and using them to turn my spoken evidence into gibberish. I wasn't the elegant lady I thought I was at all; I was that kid again, that street brat who was found alone in a hovel.

Chapter 5
The Hovel

Omni didn't scare me: I remembered being alone; I remembered how I had survived. I remembered the happy little girl who thought the world was great and that true evil only existed in fairy stories.

Omni kept his line of questioning to the 'hovel I was found in' and the fact that I had been left there on my own. 'Your mother rejected you, didn't she?' he said again. His words were harsh and angry. 'Admit it,' he demanded. I looked towards the judge – my eyes were welling up with tears; surely he would intervene – but his head was down, busily writing every word.

'No, that isn't true, no.' I was trying to speak, but the words would not come out because my mouth was so dry. I lifted the plastic cup to my lips, but only a few drops of water remained. I tried to attract the usher's attention, but he ignored me. I held the plastic beaker out towards him, but again he looked away. Fortunately, my own barrister noticed my distress and rushed forward to refill my cup with water. I gulped it down and pulled my father's handkerchief from my sleeve to dab the tears from my eyes. It was soaked by now. I had been so determined not to cry. I looked directly at my inquisitor. 'My parents were poor, they weren't animals.'

I remembered when my mother had been at home with me and

Colin, when we first moved into the bedsit in Whitton. Dad and Mum had come out to Ireland to bring us home to England in a blaze of glory, but they had a big row on the boat coming back over and Mum threw our suitcases overboard. We went our separate ways when we got to London: Colin went with Dad and I went with Mum, but then Colin came back with us when Mum found the bedsit in Whitton. Colin couldn't stay with Dad because men's digs didn't accept kids, especially not Irish ones, and Dad couldn't hide him from his landlord any more.

I remembered the 'hovel' clearly, a dirty bedsit with a dirty kitchen and a two-ring electric fire that worked if you put 6d. in the meter, and a dirty communal toilet with torn-up sheets of newspaper, if anyone bothered to put them out, instead of toilet paper. But mostly there were finger streaks of poo on the cold concrete, once-whitewashed walls. I remembered it well.

My heart had sunk when I first saw the place. It was filthy and full of rubbish, with dirty nappies strewn across the floor. I hated it and started to cry. I missed our beautiful bungalow, Bramdene, where we had last lived together as a family. But Mum said it would be OK, we would clean it up, and so we did. Mum made it sound like an adventure, and we bought a broom and a bottle of Jeyes Fluid, and she kept saying 'Jeyes Fluid' in a funny voice so Colin and I got the giggles. We scrubbed the room from top to bottom, laughing and joking as we got rid of every trace of dirt from the previous occupants, and when we finished it was bare but it was clean.

'The place was disgusting, was it not?' Omni repeated. 'One room with a sofa bed that you shared with your mother and brother, and meat lying on the floor.'

'I remember a bed, my brother had a bed,' I pleaded. I didn't know why, it didn't really make it sound any better, but my mother had not long been dead and I couldn't bear to hear his haughty, sneering words.

Life was OK at the bedsit in Whitton, but Dad wasn't living with us. It was just me, Colin and Mum. We had just come back from

Ireland. Dad didn't want Mum to know where he lived, but he would send us £4 a week in the post. When the envelope arrived, me and Colin would try to grab it first so we could pinch a ten-bob note and hide it to buy some food, because otherwise Mum would take it and disappear for a couple of days with the money and forget to leave us any food. She sometimes used to bring us back treats, and one day she came home with her handbag stuffed full of paper money. It was like something out of the films, I had never seen so much money, and the three of us pulled it all out and threw it up into the air and danced and sang with pure joy.

She had been to a casino with one of her man friends, and she laughed as she told us that they wouldn't let her in because she was wearing trousers, but it was a trouser suit so she took the trousers off and wore the long jacket as a dress. Minidresses and miniskirts were all the rage, so she got away with it. She had been playing roulette and she kept winning and there was so much money she didn't even count it, she just stuffed it in her bag. She bought steaks and cooked them for us, and she took us to the pictures to see *A Funny Thing Happened on the Way to the Forum*, and we were laughing so much that when we came out we joined the queue to go in and see it again. We went the next day, too, and we learned all the lines and could pull all the funny faces. She bought us clothes, too, and proper vests and pants and shoes: parcels galore used to turn up from the lady upstairs's catalogue. I found a place where I could have a bath at the local swimming pool. You had to queue up with your towel and pay thruppence, but you could fill the bath right up to the top with steaming hot water and lie in it for ages.

Mum took me and Colin along to the local Catholic primary school, St Edmund's, to get us signed in as new pupils, as we had just moved to the area. The headmistress and the school secretary showed us round the school, and it had lovely, clean, bright classrooms and the wonderful smell of school dinners and happy, laughing children queuing up. I remember the headmistress and the secretary being helpful and friendly. They accepted Colin straight away because Mum had his baptism certificate, but she couldn't find mine.

Then they asked us to wait outside, and they spoke in the office. They kept coming in and out and looking at us, and then wandering off again. I sat there, biting my lip like I always did when I was nervous. I could feel tears in my eyes, because I was so desperate to be allowed to join with Colin; we had been together in our first school, and it seemed so unfair. Mum kept looking at me as if to say 'Don't you dare cry', and I didn't blame her, because I knew what I was like, but the tears were welling up and I could feel myself building up to a great big howl. She shook her fist at me behind their backs, but it wasn't working and I couldn't hold it in any longer, and Colin was looking at me and poking his tongue out, and I wanted to smash his face in. There it was, I was roaring like a banshee, full-blown sobs and tears pouring down my face. I could see that Mum wanted to give me a whack, but before she could reach over the nice lady in a suit had grabbed me and sat me on her knees. I was rubbing my eyes and trying to speak between gulps. I would be good, I promised, if only they would let me come there. 'We'll sort something out, don't worry,' said the kind lady as she comforted me. She picked me up and held me close, patting my back with my head on her shoulder. Mum was apologising while looking daggers at me, and Colin was sitting there acting all innocent, so in between tears I poked my tongue out at him and made a boss-eyed face to annoy him. 'We'll arrange a baptism,' said the kind lady, 'so you'll be OK and you can start with Colin.'

I was happy then, because I was going to school and I made friends and I loved it. And I had dinner tickets, too, and I could have a meal every day. I always got seconds.

My mum made a friend, too: Gloria, who lived in the flat upstairs. Mum never usually bothered with ordinary people, because they were way beneath her, and she never had any other female friends that I could remember. But Gloria was good fun, and she had a young sister who became my friend. I remember her being in our bedsit one night, and she and Mum were drinking and laughing. She had some playing cards with pictures of naked ladies on them and they both thought it was hilarious. I was lying on the floor in front of the fire reading my comics, and I heard Gloria say the ladies on the cards were prostitutes. I didn't know what a prostitute was, so I asked them. Gloria answered that they were 'ladies who went with men to get money'. I thought about it for a moment, then I asked Mum if she was a prostitute.

Within a split second, she changed: she went into a rage like none I had ever seen before and she hit me full in the face with her fist. She grabbed at my beloved pile of comics, throwing them up into the air and ripping them to shreds, while hitting and kicking me with all her might. Colin was screaming at her to stop, but Gloria just sat there and carried on drinking. I managed to run for the door, but she slammed it and threw me down on the ground. I lay on the ground and tried to curl into a ball to deflect the blows, but I felt dizzy and faint. I could hear Colin crying and begging, 'Please, Mum, please, you're going to kill her.' Eventually, she stopped, and I lay still on the ground, afraid to move in case she started again.

'It's your fault. You make me so angry,' she shouted, and she grabbed her handbag, chucked some clothes in a case and walked towards the front door. 'You kids, you'll be the death of me,' she shouted as she slammed the door behind her. We were on our own again.

Colin helped me get into his bed. He never let me sleep in his bed, so I knew he felt sorry for me. He said he would be my servant for the next few days, and I could have anything I wanted.

We didn't go to school the next day, or the day after that, or the day after that. We knew when the school board man was knocking at the door, because we would climb onto the top of the built-in cupboard and there was a small window where we could peep out but no one could see us. The school board man used to visit in the mornings, and after he'd gone we would go to the park and play there for hours, even until it was dark. The other kids would all get called in for their tea, but not us; we could stay as long as we wanted. Colin had his friends and I had mine, and sometimes Colin would go home with one of his mates and have tea with them. Then he started staying there overnight. I wasn't jealous: I didn't want to be taken in by anyone; I wanted to stay in the park until I was the last one there. And besides, now I had Colin's bed, too.

'There was meat on the floor,' Omni said again, his voice raised to convey shock and horror. But I smiled at the memory of that: I knew there was meat on the floor – I had put it there. I had made friends with a stray cat and when we had food, I would follow the cat around and feed it to him by hand, or just leave it beside him if he wasn't hungry, so he could eat it later. I didn't have a bowl for him.

It was true I had ended up living in the bedsit on my own when they found me, but I wasn't going to admit that to Omni. I was eight or nine years old at the time. My mother would come back occasionally, usually when she was drunk and her conscience troubled her, or when she had fallen out with her latest man. I didn't mind as long as I had my comics, and if I didn't have money for the fire or the electricity I would snuggle up in Colin's bed with my little cat and read my comics by candlelight. I was always happy if I had something to read. I can't really remember where the cat had come from; I don't know if I found him or he found me. I suppose we were both strays. He didn't have a name.

Mum had left me the family allowance book and had signed all the pages so I could collect it every week. Only thirty bob, I think, but it seemed like a fortune when I picked it up. I knew I had to feed myself and the cat, so I would buy one carton of cream and three packets of Dream Topping, because we both liked that. Then I would walk miles and miles to a shop that sold out-of-date comics for half price, and I would buy loads and a Fab ice lolly to eat on the way home. As a special treat for the cat, I would sometimes go to the pet shop on the corner and buy him a slab of meat. He would eat it greedily and then lie beside me, purring. I knew he liked the meat better than the Dream Topping, but I rarely had money to buy it. Sometimes Mum came home with cash, or even jewellery, and she would leave it behind and go off again. One time she brought home a small box with a dark-blue velvet lining containing individually wrapped gold sovereigns. She had probably stolen them; I knew what she was like.

I used the coins to buy cat food. The first time I took a gold sovereign into the pet shop, the man there was very generous. He gave me a huge slab of meat and the cat was happy for days. The next time, he was not so generous. He said one coin was not enough, and he asked me if I had more at home, or anything else of value. I found a ring, an emerald surrounded with diamonds. Mum had chucked it across the road when she was arguing with her latest boyfriend. I wished and wished that she didn't drink, because she did such stupid things. I waited until she fell asleep, then I went out to search for it. I found it in the gutter and tore a page out of one of my precious comics to wrap it up and hide it away. I could get quite a lot of cat food for that. I knew she didn't care about it, probably wouldn't even remember it. But I knew the pet shop man would trade it, so I hid it away with the last of the coins.

I liked this latest man she had in her life, and she actually introduced me to him. He bought me two small teddy bears, one pink and one blue, so I liked him immediately. I had no toys or any precious belongings; all had been lost along the way in the moonlight flits as we hastily moved from place to place, gathering whatever we could carry and fleeing before the bailiffs arrived. She had bought me some new clothes via a catalogue, a Cathy McGowan bright-green velvet trouser suit and a navy-blue Cathy McGowan coat with a small cape. It was meant for an eight year old, but it was still too big – I was very small for my age, probably because I only had Dream Topping and Fab ice lollies to eat. But I loved the clothes anyway, and I went along with the story she'd given her boyfriend. I was 'away' at school most of the time and only visited for holidays and weekends. Mum could put on an amazing posh accent that made people cower in her presence, with no hint of Irish and no hint of the poverty that was our real life. She was very convincing.

She had taken me out with them for a meal, and I was the snooty public school girl, home on my hols, just like the Four Marys in my comics. I was used to Mum's posh act and even enjoyed it sometimes, but that night she was behaving appallingly and I cringed as she went into overdrive with her posh accent and her fake, superior air of snobbery. I could have cried when the waiter removed the wonderful plate of steak, chips, mushrooms and tomatoes from in front of me to be cooked a bit more. It was a feast. 'Linda doesn't like her steak too rare,' Mum insisted. Well, Linda was so hungry she could have sunk her teeth into a live cow's arse, truth be told, but I kept quiet and took another sip of my Coke, hoping and praying that the meal would be brought back. 'You must never show that you are poor, and you must never, ever show that you are hungry,' she drummed into me when we got home. 'That gives them power,' she said.

I hung on her words, and a few of her well-timed thumps around the lug knocked out all the lingering traces of Irish from my accent, and I got the occasional kick up the arse if I dared to use cockney slang. She was a formidable woman, strong, beautiful and quite, quite mad. She wasn't scared of anyone or anything, and lack of money never stopped her from doing anything that she wanted to do. She was so completely different from any other mother I had ever met. She had had my brother at 16 and me at 17, and she viewed the world through the eyes of a mischievous child.

There was a knock on the door one morning so loud that I couldn't ignore it. Bang, bang, bang, it was deafening, and I thought that whoever it was was about to break the door down. I was on my own again, so I quickly climbed up onto the top of the cupboard to see who it was. There were scary-looking policemen and other men in uniform, and unfortunately this time they saw me. 'Open the door or we'll break it down,' they said. I climbed down from the cupboard and opened the door. The men pushed in past me and demanded to know where the cat was. One of them had a cage. I ran back into the flat. The cat was hiding in the corner of the kitchen, and I picked him up and clung onto him. 'Give me the cat,' the RSPCA man said.

'No,' I shouted, 'he's my cat!'

The men were looking around, disgusted at the open tins and the rotting food. 'Come on, love, you can't keep him,' said the policeman as he gently prised the cat from my arms.

'Please, mister, please,' I begged. I felt as though my heart would break as they placed the cat into the cage. And then they left. Now I was totally alone.

I crouched down on the dirty kitchen floor, overwhelmed with sobs, unable to stop the tears as they poured down my face. As it started to get dark, I went into the other room and climbed into Colin's bed. I was still gulping back tears, but my eyes were dry; I didn't have any left. I crawled deep into the bed, pulling the covers over my head. It was pitch dark and I had no electricity. I held the two teddy bears close and cried some more, because I had given the blue one to the cat so we had one each, but now the cat would be lost and lonely, and I wished I had given it to the men for him. I had more tears now, and they felt hot on my cheeks, but I just lay there and sobbed quietly because I didn't want the nosy cow upstairs to hear me. I don't know how long I lay there. Night became day and day became night again, but still I wouldn't move. I heard the school board man knocking, but I didn't move. I didn't care.

I didn't want to bump into any of my friends, because they would ask me about the cat. I always told them stories about the cat; I said he could do loads of things that he couldn't really. I used to make it up, because I was great at telling stories, but now I didn't have anything to talk about.

'Toro, little bull, you're a silly little bull, you're a pretty little bull, but you're my little bull.' I could hear my mum's voice as I drifted in and out of dreams. I remembered sitting on my mother's knee. 'You're a brave little bull.' She would sing her version of Tommy Steele's 'Little White Bull', and I would giggle and beg her to sing it to me again. 'You're my little bull, you're a brave little bull.' The song jingled in my head until I fell into a deep, deep sleep.

Chapter 6

Omni Is Winning

Omni's words hurt me to the core; they were unbelievably cruel. I had loved my mum and she had loved me, and nothing he could say would change that. In black and white, in a hushed courtroom, it all sounded so bad. I didn't want their pity; I had hated pity all my life. It was the one emotion guaranteed to make me angry. I hated people tilting their heads and nodding sympathetically and telling me they understood when I knew darn well that they didn't. I didn't want anyone to pity me; I wanted them to admire me, I wanted them to say, 'Blimey, you went through all that, and look at what you've achieved.' I knew it was very little, in truth. I had achieved the academic qualifications I had wanted, I had two wonderful sons, but I didn't have a bean to my name. I had spent several decades navel-gazing, avoiding reality and asking, 'Why, why, why?' With my court case, I felt as though this was my moment, my time to step up to the plate. The case had long since stopped being about me; I was speaking for others too, those whose lives had been so damaged that they would never be able to face a court appearance – lives cut short by mind-altering substances that blurred out the painful memories and the fear of being so powerless again.

Standing there in the witness box, my time had come. I could speak, and I would speak, if only I could get the words out. I was not going to be silenced by the claustrophobic atmosphere of the courtroom or the cruelty of the questioning. I imagined Omni was used to breaking witnesses down, probably all before lunch, too. I looked at him defiantly, my chin raised. I knew the truth. He wasn't going to break me.

Omni continued with questions about 'the hovel'. He had hit a tender spot, and he was twisting the knife. I was losing the battle but was not yet ready to roll over. I had come through my experience at Whitton; I had pulled around. I didn't think anything else in the world could have been worse than having my cat taken away, but I was to find out that it could indeed be. However, I could survive it, I could be strong again.

My mind went back to that night in the bedsit when the cat was taken away, and how I had lain there, curled up in the dark. It was one of my worst memories. I had cried so much that only sobs and hiccups would come out. There had never been a worse tragedy in the whole history of the world. But I recovered, and I knew that as long as I lived I would never feel such deep sorrow again.

I don't know how long I lay there, but I eventually stirred when I heard post falling through the letter box. I hadn't been bothered about food; there was no point because I didn't have any money and the cat was gone. I grew excited when I picked up the envelope. It had my dad's writing on it, and I knew it would contain cash. As I tore it open, four pound notes fell out and I gasped with delight. It was a fortune. I held my head high as I walked past the pet shop. I wanted to wave the money in the owner's face and poke my tongue out at him, but I didn't, because Mum said it hurt people more if you just stuck your nose in the air.

I half ran up to the shops, and I knew exactly what I was going to get. I was going to buy new comics, not old ones, with stories that were right up to date. I knew I would have missed all the in-between stories, but I could go and get those later. I was used to catching up and I stored all my comics in date order, so I could read them the right way round the next time, and the time after that. I bought a big pot of double cream to eat when I got home and a bob's worth of penny chews, half and half of blackjacks and fruit salads. The lady in the post office looked at me a bit funny when I asked for ten bob's worth of sixpences. I needed them for the telly and for the electric fire, but her look told me that she didn't believe a scruffy little kid like me had ten bob, so I held the note up so she could see it.

Then I went to the newsagent's, where I selected my comics carefully, flicking through them to make sure they were new stories and not old ones that I had already read. 'Oi, you're not supposed to read them until you've paid for them,' shouted the man behind the counter.

'I can pay,' I said in my poshest voice, and I showed him one of my pound notes. 'See!' He shut up then and told me I could take as long as I liked. He probably thought I was a posh kid with all that money.

I didn't bother with a Fab lolly, because I was so hungry I just wanted to eat the cream. As I headed towards home, I tried to read one of my comics and dip my finger in the cream at the same time – I was so excited, I didn't know what to do first. I could never get over the thrill of a new comic, stories that I hadn't read before. I would flick through with my eyes half closed in case I glimpsed bits and spoiled it for later when I could read it properly. I loved Dennis the Menace and Minnie the Minx and the Bash Street Kids, and especially Lord Snooty. I would read the stories quickly, because I was always desperate to know what happened next; then I would read them over again slowly, giggling at the funny expressions on the characters' faces. Suddenly, I felt guilty about the cream, because I was eating it all on my own. I always bought cream because it was something the cat loved just as much as I did, and I would share it with him. Now he was gone, I felt bad eating all of it by myself, and a little bit sick.

I had decided to go back to school the next day, and I was going to get up extra early so I could buy a troll. They were all the rage at school, ugly little plastic creatures with shocks of brightly coloured hair that you could comb. They came in all colours: blue, fluorescent green, pink, yellow. Everyone was collecting them and some kids had the whole set, but I didn't even have one. I got to the shop early and bought three! A purple one, a pink one and a yellow one. I couldn't wait to show my friends. I bought a box of Maltesers, too, a whole box that I was going to eat all to myself. That would show them.

As I lined up for class the next day, the teacher called my name and said the headmistress wanted to see me. The other kids were all staring and I knew they were gloating because they thought I was in trouble. Kids always liked to see other kids in trouble, but they would have wet themselves if it had been them who had been called out.

The headmistress asked me if I had a note for my absence, and I said, 'No, Miss.' Then she demanded to know why not. I said my mum had burned her hand and she couldn't write and my dad had gone to work. Then she asked me where Colin was. I had to think about that for a minute, and I said he was at my aunt's because my aunt was having a baby and she needed his help. I didn't know where Colin was, and I hadn't seen any of our aunts for a long, long time, but I couldn't think of anything else to say.

'Tell your mother I want to see her,' the headmistress said. She wasn't being kind any more, and as I went to leave her office I heard her say to the secretary, 'I never believe a word that child says.' I think she wanted me to hear her, because she didn't lower her voice. 'And you have missed all your catechism classes too, so you are to stay in every playtime and catch up.'

'I have trolls!' I wanted to scream. It was so unfair.

'Where is your catechism book?' she demanded. I looked in my bag – I knew it wasn't there, but I just pretended. She was getting angrier and angrier and I thought she was going to hit me, but instead she grabbed me by the arm, led me to an empty classroom and told me to sit down and keep quiet. I had a little play with my trolls when she left the room. I had to keep them down under the desk in case she came back in and saw them, because I knew she would take them away if she caught me playing with them.

When she came back to the classroom, she slammed the small, black catechism book in front of me and told me to learn it, every bit of it, and I would be tested for it when she came back with Mr Beanstalk. I can't remember what his real name was, but it sounded like beanstalk and he looked like one, too. We were all scared of him because he always had a ruler in his hand and if you got the words wrong he would hit you on the knuckles with it.

'Who made you?'

'God made me.'

'Why did God make you?'

'God made me to be good and to . . .' I couldn't remember the rest. I didn't see the ruler coming, he had hidden it behind his back, but he slammed it down onto the back of my hands every time I stumbled over the words. I couldn't remember why God made me, and him hitting me wasn't helping. Again, he slammed the ruler down. I glared at him in defiance. Why did this religious stuff have to hurt so much?

I looked at Omni as he slammed his papers down onto the bench in front of him. He was playing mind games with me. Like an accomplished thespian, he owned that courtroom. It was his home ground, his territory, and the judge was his old mucker who understood exactly where he was coming from. They had seen it all before, they had heard it all before; for them, it was all so tiresome.

I had fantasised about the trial so many times, but the reality of it was entirely different. I was the one on trial, accused of having the worst parents in the world and the worst childhood imaginable prior to being saved by the nuns. It was a cruel ruse by anyone's standards, but it hit home, and it hurt. Like so many people who have had 'the convent experience', I spent many years estranged from my mother. It took adulthood, an education and the love of my dear friends to reunite me with her, and I mourned all those years we had been apart. She was still 'mad, bad and dangerous to know' right up until the end, I am delighted to say.

I knew what Omni was doing, though I was surprised that even he would do it. He wanted to destroy any or every happy memory I had ever had. I felt horribly vulnerable. I needed that girl from the past; I had never needed her more.

Chapter 7

Going into Care

....

Omni had wanted to prove what a happy, well-adjusted child I was at the convent, and he had the evidence: the records were there in front of me in black and white. As I reached page 724, I read the report of Miss Bradshaw. 'Colin and Linda are bright, happy children, and have settled in well,' she had written. The report related to her first visit to us at the convent.

The papers were so voluminous that it was apparent I would face a second day in the witness box. I was shattered. I was so shocked at seeing this report, all these years later and without being forewarned, that my head began to spin. It felt like being handed the body of a child, only to realise that the child is yourself. I flicked the pages forward, trying to read and take in as much as I could. Omni would have to wait. I was still reeling at seeing this 'tragic history of my childhood' for the very first time. Yes, it did say that 'Colin and Linda are bright, happy children'. And we were. Despite everything we had been through we were relatively unscathed, and that is how we appeared to Miss Bradshaw on her visit.

How Colin and I came to the convent was a long story. We were both taken into care after Mum abandoned the Whitton bedsit, although I don't quite remember how it happened. I remember the cat being taken away, but for some reason I don't remember them taking me. One of my first memories after leaving Whitton was attending a court hearing.

'You're not having my kids!' Mum had screamed over and over as she stood in the witness box all those years ago. Colin and I both looked down at the floor. We were dressed really smartly and were sitting in the pews of the courtroom with Miss Bradshaw between us. We had seen Dad before we went in and he told us to keep our heads down and not to worry, everything would be all right. He said, 'Whenever something bad happens, something good happens after.' He told us we would be OK. We would have proper meals every day, proper beds to sleep in and we would go to school. We knew Dad never, ever lied, so we believed him. Besides, we knew that Mum was just copying Cathy from *Cathy Come Home* – she did things like that. It was a drama that had been on telly, about a young family torn apart by poverty and homelessness, and everyone was talking about it, especially Mum. Of course, I didn't really know what it was about then, I just knew Mum loved the bit when Cathy screamed, 'You're not having my kids!' Mum was just being Cathy, wasn't she?

She had backcombed her thick black hair so much that it moved about independently like crazy dark candyfloss, tossing around in the air as she jutted her chin forward and screamed obscenities at the judge and the lawyers. The black of her mascara and eye pencil streaked down her cheeks, and she didn't look beautiful any more, she looked bedraggled and pathetic. 'They're my kids and you're not having them!' she yelled as a couple of security men tried to drag her out of the witness box, but she hung onto the wooden panel for dear life; she wasn't going without a fight.

I could feel the tears welling in my eyes, and I couldn't hold them in any longer. I fought to climb out of the pews, but I was hemmed in by Miss Bradshaw on one side and a faceless suit on the other. 'Leave my mum alone!' I screamed, and I tried to climb over the bench in front. I was desperate to reach her. 'Mum, Mum!' I cried. I wanted to run to her; I wanted those pigs to take their hands off her. Miss Bradshaw had caught me and was struggling to hold me back.

'No, Linda, no,' Colin said, and he tried to grab my arm even though he was crying too, but I didn't care. Miss Bradshaw was holding me tightly, her arms clasped around my waist, but I kept kicking and lashing out.

'My mum, my mum, I want my mum,' I kept screaming as I watched them dragging her out of the courtroom. She had a security man either side of her, hanging onto her arms, forcing her to walk forwards, but she kept looking back and she was shouting, 'Colin! Linda!' She was calling out to us. 'I want my kids, I want my kids,' she was screaming to anyone who would listen. She was struggling to break away from the vice-like grip of the security men, fighting to get away from them, but it was impossible and we could hear her huge sobs echoing through the sombre halls as they dragged her away.

Miss Bradshaw was still hanging onto me and I was still screaming. I hated them, all of them; I wanted to kill them. 'Let me go!' I kept screaming. 'Get off me, get off me, I want my mum.' Dad was sitting in the benches on the other side, and he pushed past everyone to get to me.

'Let her go!' he shouted angrily at Miss Bradshaw and the others who had joined in to grab my arms and legs to stop me lashing out. 'I said let her go!' Dad was furious, and as I felt them release their grip I ran into his arms and felt as though my heart would break. He carried me out of the courtroom and sat down with me on his knee, holding me close to him as my hysterical crying softened to hiccupping sobs. I buried my head into his shoulder as he soothed my tears, and Colin stood beside us, snuggled up with Dad's other arm protectively around him, drawing him in close, so the three of us were together.

Miss Bradshaw, the social workers and the court officials hovered close by, waiting to step in, but Dad glared at them with a look that said 'back off'. 'It's going to be OK,' he said softly, as he held us both close to him. 'You know what your mother's like. She'll be all right,' he assured us. 'You'll probably see her next week,' he said, smiling, 'and right as rain she'll be.'

We sort of knew that it was just Mum being daft, but there, in that place, it was frightening, and we didn't know what they were going to do to her and I wanted those horrible men to take their hands off her and to stop hurting her, and I wanted to hit them and kick them, and I wanted to poke my tongue out at the judge and tell him to feck off and leave my mum alone, but I couldn't because they had stopped me. I felt so helpless.

Dad stroked my hair and said, 'I know, I know.' He understood my anger and he understood my tears, and he pulled his hanky out from his pocket and used it to wipe the tears from my face. Then he held it to my nose and told me to blow. 'You've always got a blooming snotty snozzle,' he teased, and I found myself laughing, even though I didn't want to.

Chapter 8
Campbell Road, Twickenham

....

The first children's home I was put into after I had been found in the bedsit in Whitton was a foster home in Campbell Road, Twickenham. Once again, Colin and I hadn't been going to school and the school board man used to knock on the door regularly. We used to hide from him. Dad wasn't living with us there, but I think he suspected what was going on and contacted the authorities. He was concerned because we hadn't been going to school, and that no one was looking after us.

I was placed in Campbell Road and Colin in a reception centre in Richmond. The reception centre was for bad boys, boys who had committed crimes or run away. Colin hadn't done anything wrong, but there wasn't room for him at Campbell Road and they had nowhere else to send him.

I loved the foster home in Campbell Road. It was made up of two large 1930s semis knocked into one and it was run by two elderly spinsters, Miss Smith and Miss Jones, who wore polyester housecoats over their clothes and spoke softly. It was always warm and comfortable and always smelled of washing powder and home cooking, and the two 'aunties' were kind and thoughtful.

I didn't want to speak when I arrived there; I didn't know why, there wasn't really anything to be afraid of. The aunties seemed kind and Miss Jones took me upstairs to show me where I would be sleeping. When she showed me my bed, I wanted to cry. It was in a room with three others, and it had crisp white sheets, clean blankets and a pink cover like the others. There was also a wooden chair and a locker. The floor was wooden, too, and highly polished, with a small rug next to each of the beds.

'You can put your things in the locker,' Miss Jones said to me kindly, but I just looked at the clean bed and my bottom lip started to tremble. She put her arm around my shoulders and tried to comfort me, but I was all right and held the tears back. Yet still I wouldn't speak. 'Come on,' she said, 'let's sort you out with a towel and some wash things.' She then led me to a huge cupboard filled with a neat stack of laundered towels, brand-new toothbrushes still in their packets and new bars of soap and toothpaste, and she gave me a flannel and soapbox to keep my own soap in. I held the flannel and the soapbox in my hand, unsure whether they really were for me, afraid that she might take it all back. She was confused by my silence and my sad face. 'You can have a different one if you want,' she said. I hung onto the soapbox and the flannel; I didn't want to let go. The flannel was clean, but it wasn't brand new, and she thought it was the flannel that was troubling me. She reached into the cupboard again. 'Here,' she said, 'this one is brand new,' offering me a new white one that she had pulled from the back. I didn't want the new one; I wanted the old one that she had given me, and I wasn't letting go.

She then led me to the bathroom and started to run a bath. 'I'll sort you out a nightdress and a dressing gown,' she said, 'and I'll see if I can find you some slippers, then you can come downstairs and have supper with the others.' Still I wouldn't speak. Everything was so clean and tranquil, I felt as though I was in a dream. She was a kind lady and I didn't want to hurt her feelings, but I was filled with a morbid dread, as though everything was going to go horribly wrong at any moment. 'Do you want me to help you wash your hair?' she asked.

'No,' I snapped.

She laughed. 'So you have got a voice,' she said.

The bath was luxurious, but still I was filled with dread. The beautiful bubbles soon turned to mucky scum as I scrubbed away the layers of dirt and grime. Miss Jones had laid out a nightdress and dressing gown on 'my' bed, and a clean vest and pants, and she had placed a brush and comb on top of the locker. I quickly put on the nightclothes, breathing in the delicious newly laundered fragrance; then I picked up the brush and comb and tugged to pull the knots out of my hair. I looked out of the bedroom window and I could see a church steeple in the distance and rows of large, neat suburban houses, and I wondered where I was and who these people were and I wondered where Colin was, and my mum and dad, and would I ever see them again.

I sat on the bed and waited, taking in the clean and pleasant room, noting the dolls and teddy bears on the other beds and wondering who slept in them. I was still fighting back tears, but I was determined not to cry, not to say anything. Mum had told me never to tell anyone our business. 'Keep quiet,' she said. 'You mustn't say a word, and I will come and get you.' But I didn't know if she would this time, because she didn't know where I was. And I liked it there, and I liked the ladies and the nice things they had given me, and I didn't want anyone to take it all away. I made up my mind that I would never speak again.

Miss Jones came back upstairs to get me and she led me down to join the others. 'It's OK if you don't want to speak,' she said. 'You can speak when you're ready.' She gently squeezed my hand. 'This is the playroom,' she said as she led me into the large front room where all the other children were sitting in their dressing gowns, all pink and clean and freshly scrubbed. They smelled of soap and talcum powder and they were drinking cocoa, eating biscuits and laughing and chatting. Some of the bigger kids were sitting at the large table playing board games and giggling. 'We have lots of games,' Miss Jones said, and she opened a large cupboard filled with boxes and boxes of toys and games. 'And we have books, too.' My eyes lit up at the sight of the bookcase: it was full of books, big ones, small ones, hardbacks and pop-up ones. I was in awe. Then she led me through a door in the playroom that went into the other house and the other front room. That front room was the dining room, she said. It had two large tables, and a couple of the kids were putting out knives and forks and spoons and plates. 'That's for breakfast tomorrow morning,' said Miss Jones.

After she had shown me around the house, she took me back to the playroom and brought me some cocoa. The other kids were trying to talk to me, they kept asking my name and where I had come from. I kept quiet, even though they were being friendly. I liked the house and I liked them, but I was afraid, even if I didn't know what I was afraid of. I loved the feel of the crisp white sheets and the sheer comfort of the bed, and I lay there and cried, afraid to be comfortable, afraid that it might all be taken away.

Best of all, I started at a new school. Kneller Girls' School in Twickenham was my first secondary school, and I was in awe at the sheer size and scale of the buildings and the facilities. Our uniform was grey: a grey pleated skirt or gymslip that went over a crisp white blouse, a grey and red tie and a grey blazer with the school's emblem on the pocket. Miss Smith and Miss Jones delighted in kitting me out, and they both proudly accompanied me to the school shop and ordered everything I could possibly need: five blouses, three gymslips, one tie, one blazer, an assortment of PE stuff for playing hockey and horrendous big black pants and a white polo shirt for gym. I was so small and skinny that even the smallest of the regular pleated skirts drowned me, coming down to my ankles, which made all three of us hoot with laughter. The cuffs of the blazer went down past my fingertips, and the padded shoulders stood up on their own, seemingly detached from the little body underneath.

I stood out like a sore thumb on the day that I started. New kids are always easy to spot: their uniforms are immaculate and usually way too big for them. Friendships had already been made and groups had been formed, and I could see that Miss Jones felt for me as she waved me off at the school gates. I clutched my brown satchel close to me, comforted by the smell of the leather and secure in the knowledge that it contained pencils, a notepad, a ruler, a geometry set and a real fountain pen. I had never had such luxuries before, and simply by owning them I felt safe and unafraid.

It was impossible to stay sad at Campbell Road – the ladies were so kind and the children were so happy. I especially loved the mealtimes. Miss Jones would sit at the head of one table and Miss Smith at the head of the other, and we always had teacups and saucers and a big pot of tea in the middle of each table and we could have as many cups as we wanted. And we always had bread and butter and jam. Apricot jam was Miss Jones's favourite, so it was my favourite, too.

I was a first year and I was put into Form 1B, a class full of lively and brightish 11-year-old girls – not quite as brainy as 1A but not as daft as 1D. I tried to endear myself to the other girls in the class, but I was several months too late. In girls' schools, two is cosy, three is a crowd and four upwards is a gang, with leaders and a strict pecking order, where newcomers are only welcome if they are happy to stay on the bottom rungs and keep their mouths shut.

I kept myself to myself at school, still luxuriating in the sheer bliss of waking up to find fresh new clothes each day, eating a wonderful cooked breakfast with lashings of tea and toast and marmalade, and being warmly sent off to school by the aunties. I was so excited by the school, with its intricate maze of corridors that led to science laboratories and art rooms and libraries, and it tickled me that when the bell sounded we all had to pack up our books and move to the next classroom, passing other forms as we all rushed in single file through the corridors.

I think the school was Protestant, because I soon found out that you didn't have to attend assembly if you had a different religion. For the first time in my life, I realised I could claim to be a Roman Catholic and get something good out of it. While the others were all herded off to assembly, I stayed behind in the form room with the other heathens, where we could study, catch up on our homework or simply mess about, because there was no one to supervise us. Our form teacher tried to persuade me that it really wouldn't impact on my Catholicism too much if I attended assembly – after all, there wasn't that much between Catholicism and the Church of England, she said – but I wouldn't be swayed: principles are principles and all that. Besides, I needed that time in the morning to do the homework that I hadn't done the night before. But, of course, I didn't mention that.

The science laboratory was set out like a university lecture hall. The pupils sat in rows of benches that graduated upwards like a Roman amphitheatre while the teacher down at the front skilfully passed on the textbook facts of how the earth began. I watched and listened in awe as she explained the basis of Darwin's theory of evolution and showed us slides of fossils and dinosaurs, but I couldn't equate them with what I had learned up until then.

'What about God?' I thought to myself. 'I thought he made the world in seven days? What about Adam and Eve?' I was confused and bewildered, and the memory of the harsh raps of the ruler across my knuckles during catechism lessons were a constant painful reminder of exactly how the world began. I listened carefully to the teacher's words and drew diagrams in my science jotter, but it just didn't make sense.

'But, Miss, but, Miss . . .' I was longing to put my hand up; I wanted her to explain. Eventually, I could contain myself no longer; I desperately needed to know.

She put her chalk down and leaned back against her desk, sighing deeply, as though she were uncomfortable with my questions. 'The Bible was written a very long time ago,' she said, 'and it consists of fables, simple stories; it was a means by which to explain the world to the people who lived at that time.'

'What's a fable?' asked one of the other kids, and then she started to explain that, and then others asked stupid questions too, and the whole lesson deteriorated into a discussion of fairy stories and tales of morality that taught us how to live and I never did get the answers I was looking for.

In art lessons, we made tiny homes out of shoeboxes and covered the tiny walls with wallpaper and made tiny furniture out of cardboard. Miss Jones took me to a carpet shop to ask for a sample, so my little box had a carpet, and she helped me to make tiny curtains for the tiny windows, so it made the perfect home.

One of our lessons was calligraphy, the art of beautiful handwriting, and we had to use special pens made of wood with specially crafted nibs that you dipped in ink; they transformed your basic ABCs to proper joined-up writing with swirls and flourishes, adding a sophistication that said you were no longer at primary school. I could always copy the top line beautifully, but then I would get impatient and rush to finish it, so that my handwriting came out as spidery scribbles covered in ink blobs.

It was during these classes that I made my one and only friend at Kneller. Nicola, like me, was a loner; she had no 'special' friend and she was not part of any of the popular groups. She was a plain girl with short hair, but she had a warm and friendly personality and her kindness shone through. I had caught her looking at me sympathetically as I asked my awkward questions in lessons, or when those other girls I tried to speak to turned their backs on me.

Her calligraphy was beautiful, from the top line right down to the bottom, and she worked on it as if it were some precious art form, concentrating on each letter, paying careful attention to every detail. I so admired her skill and was so frustrated that I couldn't do it. My dad's handwriting was good, too, but my mother's was truly beautiful. Her writing flowed across the page, symmetrical yet artistic, with carefully constructed loops and tails and capital letters that began paragraphs with style and confidence. My own handwriting changed from day to day; I had no style, no symmetry, just a scribble, and if indeed I do have multiple personalities, they have always taken it in turns to do my writing for me. I think a handwriting expert could look at samples of my writing and never know that they were written by the same person.

Nicola took me under her wing; she saw me as fragile and vulnerable and in need of protection. She would rush to school ahead of me so she could meet me at the school gates, and she would fend off any bullies or teachers who simply didn't understand me. At playtime, we would sit together and chat at a hundred miles an hour: so much to say and so little time to say it. She didn't laugh or make fun of me. I told her I could sing, I told her my granny had taught me, and she said I had the voice of an angel. I sang 'Those Were the Days' by Mary Hopkin; it was in the charts at the time and I knew all the words. The aunties had put a television in the dining room so we could watch *Top of the Pops* even if we were eating our tea, and Thursday nights were so exciting: the charts meant everything, and learning the words to our favourite songs meant even more.

Dad would visit me every week, and if he got there early enough we would go and pick up Colin so the three of us could go out together. Sometimes he would go to see Colin first, and then they would come and visit me. I used to love Dad's visits because we would always go out somewhere exciting, like the pictures or ice skating. There was an ice rink in Richmond and it didn't take much to persuade Dad to take me there. He used to go skating when he was a kid in Scotland, and he was happy to put on his boots and zoom around the ice rink with all the fast ones. But he would spend ages with me as well, and he would try to hold me up, even when he knew for sure that I was going to fall over. I couldn't skate at all, even though I kept trying, and I definitely wasn't graceful like the skaters on the telly, but he would take hold of my hand and tell me I could do it. Yet he would always let me stay close to the edge so I could grab the side when I felt myself falling over. Sometimes I used to make him fall over too, but he just used to laugh and pick himself up, then pick me up, and we would have another go. Mum would visit too and take me out. We always went to the shops and she would buy me anything I wanted and give me money to hide away.

I didn't feel psychologically damaged by Campbell Road. I experienced nothing but kindness there, and I wanted Colin to be there with me. Although I didn't really like him, I missed him. The authorities didn't like to separate siblings, and eventually a place was found where we could be together. It was in St Anne's Convent, Orpington. It was over in Kent, far, far away from Whitton and far, far away from everything of the world we had ever known.

Chapter 9

St Anne's Convent: New Kids on the Block

It was a steep and bumpy road up to the convent, and I was overwhelmed by the size of the building, a huge Victorian gothic construction that stretched across the entire length of the top of the hill. Colin and I sat in the back of the taxi, quiet and unsure of where we were going. Miss Bradshaw sat in the front, neatly perched on her seat with her handbag on her knee. It had been a long and difficult journey, Miss Bradshaw in her country tweeds accompanying me and Colin and our two suitcases, struggling from train to train as we left Surrey and made our way across London to head down towards Kent.

We had piled our baggage onto a trolley at Waterloo and made our way towards the station restaurant. Miss Bradshaw had wanted to take us for a proper meal before we embarked on the second part of our journey. She ordered us pork chops with boiled potatoes and carrots, and I had never disliked a meal more. 'It smells of pigs,' I said to her.

'It's pork, Linda, just eat it up.'

'But I feel sick, Miss,' I said.

'Just shut up and eat it,' Colin said. But the pig smell was filling my nostrils, and the crashing of the plates and cutlery and all the people rushing round were making me dizzy and nauseous.

'You are just nervous, Linda, that's all. Try and eat a little bit,' Miss Bradshaw said, and she went back to fiddling with her little purse, carefully counting out the coins and writing notes in her little red cash book. I pushed the food around on the plate. There was no way I could eat it. It felt like the whole place smelled of pigs, and I was trying to hold back the vomit that I could feel rising in my throat.

The sickness and the smell of pigs were still in my nose and throat as I looked up at the huge building in front of us. Miss Bradshaw was carefully counting out the coins for the taxi driver and had told us to stand and wait. The door was huge, and Colin made me laugh because he said Herman Munster would probably open it. But it wasn't Herman Munster, it was a large lady dressed from head to foot in black with her unattractive face framed in white. Her robes were full and long, with a leather belt around her waist and, hanging down by the side, a chain of beads that rattled as she walked. She stepped forward and picked up our heavy bags as though they were filled with feathers. They looked tiny and insignificant in her huge, man-like hands. We followed her into a waiting room and sat with Miss Bradshaw, each of us perched on hard wooden chairs that you just knew would screech if you moved them one inch. I looked at Colin, hoping he would make me laugh, but he just stared down towards the floor.

There was a large wooden crucifix on the wall, with the figure of Jesus hanging there almost dead, his face and body twisted in agony, with blood oozing from his hands and his feet and his side. His eyes stared up to heaven, pleading with God to save him as the blood trickled down from his crown of thorns.

I couldn't smell the pigs any more; now all I could smell was the wax from the highly polished floors and the faint scent of incense. My sickness had been replaced with sheer terror.

A few moments later, the large nun opened the door and a much older, smaller and frailer nun walked slowly into the room. Miss Bradshaw signalled for me and Colin to stand up, and she stood up too as the large nun introduced us to Mother Ambrose. She politely shook Miss Bradshaw's hand and told her she hoped we had had a pleasant journey; then she looked down at me and Colin, smiling sweetly.

'So you are Colin and Linda,' she said. She patted Colin on the head, then gently touched my face. 'Sister Bridget will take you down to Tara. That will be your house, and you will soon feel at home.'

Sister Bridget said there was a playground, too, and other children the same age, and there was a church at the other end of the building. 'Do you like church?' she asked us. We were both too scared to answer, so Mother Ambrose asked us if we had ever been to church. She sounded a little bit shaken, horrified that we might not have been churchgoers. I answered 'yes' nervously, feeling a frog in my throat and scared that my voice wouldn't work.

'And who took you to church, dear?' she asked gently.

'My mother,' I said, but it came out as a whisper.

'And do you know how to behave in church?' Mother Ambrose asked.

'Yes, you have to shut the feck up,' I replied. My voice worked all right that time.

Miss Bradshaw said, 'Linda, Linda, Linda,' and Colin stifled a giggle.

'We don't use language like that, Linda,' said Mother Ambrose sternly, and she tutted and looked towards Sister Bridget as if to say it was time for all of us to make a move.

It was hard watching Miss Bradshaw leave. Colin and I had grown fond of her, and although she wasn't tactile or particularly affectionate, she was kind and always polite. As she made her way towards the door, I wanted to run after her and beg her to take me with her. I wanted to go back to Campbell Road, to the nice house and the nice ladies and the clean sheets and the bread and jam. It had been a warm and welcoming house and I had wanted to stay there, but I couldn't because Colin had been placed somewhere else and the authorities had wanted to keep us together and Mum had told them we were Catholics. There were so many reasons, Miss Bradshaw had told us, and St Anne's was the best place for us, a place where we would be safe and secure and could go to school every day. We both loved school, probably because we had missed so much of it, and this place was like a school but so much colder. The cold didn't come from the lack of heating; the cold came from within the very walls and from the chill that I felt in the presence of those stern and frightening women in their black and white robes.

We followed Man Hands (as I thought of Sister Bridget already) through the twisting, winding corridors that never seemed to end, our footsteps breaking the awesome silence of the formidable building: Sister Bridget with her long purposeful strides and the hurried, small footsteps of Colin and me as we tried to keep up. 'There's other houses in the building, but your house is at the far end. Tara, that's where you'll be staying,' she said in her thick Irish accent. I wondered about the houses: where were they? Where were the children? The place was silent. 'Stop dreaming and hurry along,' she snapped at me. 'And there'll be no more language like that, I can tell you. Jesus, Mary and Joseph, I've never heard such language in my life, and from a child, may God forgive you – and you had better ask God to forgive you.' She stopped and looked at me angrily. 'Hurry up!' she shouted.

The corridors were narrow, cold and oppressive, and the smell of fresh wax was overwhelming. At one point we walked through a dormitory, row upon row of small, neatly made beds in stark, bare surroundings with no signs that any human beings lived there, no personal items like there were at Campbell Road, nothing on the walls other than scary crucifixes with the blood-soaked head of Jesus looking down in sorrow. We went upstairs, we went downstairs, we went through long, winding passages and had no hope of ever finding our way back. I was bolder than Colin, so I dragged behind and looked up and around me, trying to take in the corridors, the dark vestibules, the few and far between adult-height windows that you would have to stand on a chair to see out of to catch a glimpse of the world beyond. The corridors were dark, and they possessed the hazy, shadowy quality of those spooky old black and white films in which the decapitated body of a man would appear out of the wall carrying his head under his arm. The nun kept telling me to hurry up, but still I dawdled and looked around me, always running the last few steps to catch up.

Sister Bridget allowed us to stop momentarily in a huge kitchen. She put the bags down and showed us her very own province with pride and a sense of achievement. She ran the kitchen, she said proudly, and she cooked all the meals for Mother Ambrose and all of the sisters. And she made bread, and she made soup in huge pots, and stirred them with huge wooden spoons. She swept her arms out as if to say 'all of this is my domain'. It was all silver with giant-sized pots and pans and a walk-in cupboard filled with every tin, packet and preserved food ever made. The walk-in freezer was filled with the headless corpse of a pig. My nausea was building rapidly and the smell was making my stomach churn.

I was happy to get out of the kitchen. As fascinated as I was, the whole place was crowding in on me and I felt as if I was suffocating. Eventually, we reached 'the door', the entrance into Tara. Tara would be our house, said Sister Bridget again. 'It's where you will be living,' she added, just to make sure we understood. We were standing on a landing at the top of a very small staircase – two, maybe three stairs, just enough to elevate us above the group that had come to meet us. For a second, Colin and I stared at those in front of us and they stared back, all of us trying to glean as much information as possible from the briefest glance – too short a moment to capture in words, but long enough for that moment to be held in time and stay with me for ever.

This door into Tara led into another world again. It was a building on the end of a building, independent of those miles of corridors, much lighter and more open, but still connected to the convent by a tiny door at the top of those three stairs. To the left of where we stood there was a large wooden-framed window that looked out onto a school playground. Ahead of us, there was a corridor that led off into the playroom to the left, the kitchen to the right and the dining room straight ahead. The dining room at the end had many windows and a door that led directly outside. It was at the very right end of the huge building that stretched over the hill, with Tara at one end and Holy Innocents' Church at the other.

The whole of St Anne's Convent, or orphanage, was a huge building at the top of a hill and could be seen from the main road. It was made up of several 'houses', each containing approximately 12 children of various ages, with siblings kept together and a nun as housemother and an 'uncle' as housefather. They were supposed to be like families.

The silent moment of introduction to Tara quickly passed and the reality became all too clear. In front of us stood a fierce, squat nun, dressed exactly the same as Sister Bridget but half her height and twice her width, her black robes bulging with rolls of fat and her short, stumpy arms folded and squeezed together with her fists tightly clenched. Her face was huge, round and moonlike, flushed as though she were out of breath, and her cheeks squelched out of her coif – the tight white part of her headdress that fitted tightly around her face – as it strained to hold in the mounds of quivering flesh. She had bright-blue eyes twinkling out from under fuzzy ginger eyebrows: eyes, I would soon learn, that could go from a twinkle to pure hatred in a split second. Sister Consolata, a short, rotund, red-haired nun who wore her habit with the pride of a Nazi prison guard.

I knew she was a redhead, because one time, later, as we stood in the kitchen, a lock of hair fell out of her coif, and she cut it off with a pair of scissors: a quick snip, then a fierce cutting motion across the thick chunk of bright-red hair that she squeezed in her chubby little fingers. Then she flung it into the bin. Just like that, without a moment's thought. I was horrified, because I was at an age when your hair was your shining glory, and you brushed it 100 times every night if you wanted to be like a romantic Brontë heroine. And if you liked a boy and he touched your hair gently, then you knew he liked you too. To me, the nuns were different, sort of asexual, not women at all but a strange and frightening unknown species. I suppose I must have known Sister Consolata was a woman (though I was never sure about Sister Bridget), but that stray lock of hair somehow humanised her momentarily, and she didn't seem so frightening.

Our first sight of our new home and house parents made quite a tableau. A youngish man, Uncle Peter, stood behind Sister Consolata, as though he were her husband in a wedding picture. On either side of him were two tall, dark-haired teenage boys. They all stood in exactly the same way: legs slightly apart, arms folded and fists clenched. It could easily have been a family photograph. Uncle Peter was taller than the boys and had thick, dark hair, just like them – they could have been mistaken for father and sons, or even brothers. Uncle Peter's face had strong, almost caricature-like features: large, dark eyes and full, thick lips that twisted into an obscene snarl as he spoke or tried to smile. But his voice was gentle and friendly – overly so – and his hand and arm gestures were huge and demonstrative, as though he were talking to an audience, and before long he was: he separated himself from the group and took centre stage while we all looked on.

I suppose we were an audience. Sister Consolata beckoned Sister Bridget to stay. (We were soon to find out that Consolata loved to show Uncle Peter off to the other nuns.) Sister Bridget tucked her arms under her scapula, the long, dark length of material that goes over the front and back of a nun's habit. All the nuns used them to hide their hands or to pray. The rest of the audience were the other children, who stood huddled in two rows to our right, with the bigger children standing at the back. Nearly all of them had their heads down, looking towards their feet, and some of them had their hands together, nervously twisting and pulling at their fingers. It was hard to tell the girls from the boys, because they all had the same haircuts, but the girls wore long dresses and skirts that hovered just above their ankle socks. I noticed one girl there who looked about my age, and I tried to catch her eye and hoped she would smile at me so I would have at least one friend. But she didn't dare to look up properly; she just stole glances, then quickly put her head back down as she stared at the gnarled shapes she was making with her fingers. I followed the line of her gaze until my eyes fixed on her slippers. I couldn't look away. The slippers were pink, and one of them had a bobble and one of them didn't, and I wanted to cry then, because I was sad for her, because she had lost a bobble.

Everyone listened to Uncle Peter in awe – even the younger children were now looking in his direction. The two older boys mouthed his words, as though they knew them by heart, or maybe because they were captivated by his presence and were subconsciously mimicking him. Uncle Peter had steered us all into the playroom, where he had much more room, so that we could all hear him and see him. Within moments, he was proudly glorifying the image of Tara, our house, a house that we were privileged to be in, and all the children nodded, and so did Sister Consolata as she gazed at him in adoration. And Sister Bridget was trying to make herself look smaller so she could gaze up at him too. I wondered if he was a saint.

The only saint I could think of at the moment was St Francis of Assisi, the humble monk who liked children and animals. But Uncle Peter wasn't anything like St Francis of Assisi: he was more like a Bee Gee but with shorter, dark hair, or like Jonathan King without the moustache. He wore skintight bell-bottomed trousers, a brightly coloured shirt opened almost to his waist and a bulky gold crucifix that bounced on his bulging groin when he sat on tables to tell us stories. I was sure that St Francis had taken a much more gentle approach, but Uncle Peter stood in front of us, his body rigid, then made a great display of locking his legs apart with his crotch thrust forward and his arms folded. I noticed that the two older boys did the same.

'I have suffered, more than you could ever know,' he said softly. Then he walked slowly over to the table and sat on the edge of it, his overly tight trousers straining against his thighs. Then he cupped his groin and stared up towards the window and sighed, giving us all time to reflect and share in the moment. 'I was a Jesuit monk, you know.' He looked down and sighed again. I looked around the room and saw everyone's faces were filled with sorrow. Sister Consolata even looked as though she might cry.

Then, with great emotional and physical upheaval, Uncle Peter stood up from the table, huffed and puffed, and threw himself down onto the floor to demonstrate for us his greatest humiliation as a monk, and that was prostrating himself naked in front of the altar while his fellow brothers whipped him. I was quite relieved that he kept his clothes on when he demonstrated that bit. 'Mortification of the body is good for the soul,' he said, and then he went to great pains to tell us how he would make himself suffer every day for the glory of God. His face would then take on a pious, holy look as he gazed up to the ceiling, his hands temporarily removed from his bulging groin and clasped in prayer, while the nuns whispered under their breath about what a martyr he was.

I didn't know much about religion then; I merely wondered why he would want to do that. I didn't feel sorry for him – in fact, I found him a bit creepy – but as I looked around at the adoring faces of the others, I felt as though it was just me. I felt like the odd one out, an outsider, and I felt that it was my fault, that I wasn't godly enough or pure enough.

I wanted to believe the same thing as everybody else, and sometimes I prayed to God with a vengeance, especially if something I had done wrong was about to be discovered. I tried squeezing my eyes together and saying, 'I do believe, I do believe,' like the Cowardly Lion in *The Wizard of Oz*, but nothing ever gave me that 'state of grace' that they all raved about. I had only experienced it occasionally and unintentionally, that amazing moment when you step out of the confession box 'in a state of grace', absolved of all sin, a momentary high that lasts only a split second before you have your first impure or unkind thought or you trip on a prayer mat and say, 'Oh, feck it.'

But those were the only times I ever felt trance-like about religion. I suppose at those times I felt as though I truly believed, but I was never sure whether it was only because I was getting something out of it. I couldn't see real tears on the Virgin Mary either and wasn't even going to pretend, even though Kieron Murphy* got spoiled rotten by the nuns after he said he had seen them. I did always remember to bow my head when I said the Virgin Mary's name, though – still do, out of habit.

Our introduction to St Anne's and to Tara had been so weird that on that first night I lay in bed wondering what lay in store for us. They had put me in the bed next to a girl called Molly* in the girls' dormitory and we whispered to each other long into the night. She told me all about the nuns and Uncle Peter, and she warned me to watch her and follow what she did, so I could keep out of trouble. I listened in trepidation. It sounded so frightening that I didn't believe half of what she was telling me; it sounded so unreal. The place was clean, and it was warm, and we would get three meals a day, every day: how could that possibly be bad?

'You'll see,' Molly whispered to me. 'You'll see.'

Chapter 10

I Know What You Are

I was soon to find that these weird house meetings took place every evening, and it was at these times that our wrongdoings would be revealed and punished. I was also soon to find that it was hard not to do something wrong.

Colin and I quickly adapted to the harsh routine of convent life. Uncle Peter or Sister Consolata or one of the older boys would barge into our dormitory at six every morning, sometimes earlier, shouting at us all to wake up. Then Molly and I, the two oldest girls, had to get all the little ones up, and we all had to strip out of our nightclothes and go downstairs to the playroom in our underwear to have a wash, supervised by the older boys. It was humiliating.

My pride got me into trouble within days of our arriving at the convent. I was horrified and felt degraded to find that each morning we girls and all the younger kids were dragged out of our beds and told to remove our nighties by the older boys, on the orders of Uncle Peter. We were not naked, but we had to walk down the stairs in vests and pants to the playroom and queue up to wash in the little sinks. The older boys supervised this and inspected our ears and necks to make sure that we had washed them properly with the hard green slabs of soap that we also used to scrub the floors.

I fought back for the first few days, but there was no way of 'winning' or avoiding each morning's ordeal. I endured this daily torment and spat and swore at first, but then I resolved to be silent. I had never heard of being 'insolently' silent before, but apparently it was a sin, as bad as any other, and showed wilful defiance. And, yes, there were punishments for that too.

Once we had got ourselves and the little ones ready for school, we had to run down and set the tables for breakfast. After breakfast, we all had to clear away the plates; then Molly and I had to stack the chairs on the tables so we could sweep and wash the floor. The older kids all had to make our own beds with perfect hospital corners, and Molly and I had to do the beds for the little ones as well before we could leave for school.

Coming home from school, the chores would begin again. We set the table for tea, cleaned all the kids' shoes for school the next day, had tea and then washed the dining room floor, which we had to polish until you could see your face in it. Molly and I started to take some perverse sort of pride in how shiny we could get it, as if we were trying to make the nun – we quickly took to calling Sister Consolata simply 'the nun' when she wasn't around – happy, and maybe we were, but now I feel ashamed at our pathetic attempts to crawl around her. She hated us as much as we hated her.

When the chores were done, the boys were allowed to do their homework, but the nun would always think up more chores for me and Molly so we never got a chance to do ours. I remember desperately wanting to complete an essay on *Jane Eyre* and sitting scribbling it in the toilet while all the others were asleep.

When the nun was berating me, she would always tell me that no man would ever marry me or want me, and she said if anyone was ever eejit enough, he would batter me constantly and I would deserve it. I didn't care: I didn't particularly like boys; they were annoying, like Colin. I liked my best friend, Molly, and I could talk to her about anything in the world, and she could talk to me.

We said Sister Consolata couldn't get a man and that was why she was a nun. None of the nuns were pretty. They all had cruel hatchet faces, pinched by the tight white starch of their habits. They rarely smiled, and I only ever saw Sister Consolata laugh out loud when one of us was hurt, like when Molly accidentally burned her arm getting a tray of food out of the oven.

Their behaviour was entirely different in front of 'normal' people: that is, parents, social workers and the people from outside the convent who attended Holy Innocents' Church. In front of them, they were paragons of piety, virtue and kindness. Everyone referred to them as Sister, as in 'Yes, Sister; no, Sister', and the creepy ones would half dip their heads when they said it. Even my mother spoke to them in that way, to show off what a good Catholic she was, even though she wasn't. When we first went there, every week Mum said she wanted to kill Sister Consolata, and it was really embarrassing, so we stopped telling her things. It only used to make things worse anyway, because the nun would make us suffer for it. I think that was when Sister Consolata started calling me 'Madam Hutton' – it was her way of taunting me, because I 'thought I was better than everybody else'.

I didn't think that I was better than anyone else; I just couldn't understand why they weren't bold like me. Molly was great, but she didn't seem to know that she was. I had taken a liking to Molly that first night. Uncle Peter and the nun had said she was backward and that her mum was in the loony bin, but they couldn't see her as I did. Out of their sight, she was funny and interesting and, in her own way, a little rebel. Even when we were dragged out of bed in the middle of the night and made to scrub a floor, she could make me laugh. She wasn't very good at schoolwork, reading or writing or maths, but, like me, it was probably because she had had any knowledge battered out of her by Catholic teachers. I didn't know the difference between a verb and a noun – still don't. That silly woman with a ruler was knocking it out of me, not drumming it in. But Molly wasn't stupid. She just kept quiet and pretended she was. She would walk around with her head bowed, hiding beneath a thick black fringe, her hands clasped tightly in front of her. Her fringe used to drive me demented because, being the same height as me, she had to lean her head back to speak to me. I was always trying to persuade her to try hairgrips. She was always bumping into things, but she seemed to know her way around the maze of waxed corridors going by the feel of the wear and tear of the floorboards beneath her feet. Actually, most people used to walk with their heads down through those winding corridors; well, the nuns did anyway. I think it was because they had to make the sign of the cross every time they walked past a crucifix and they probably couldn't be arsed, so they kept their heads down so they wouldn't see them.

We kids didn't count as anyone, so there was no need for the nuns to put on an act around us. We didn't even count as humans. Even if you spoke to one of them and she smiled, she would forget who you were ten seconds later. They paraded us in church as trophies of their piety and dedication, a symbol of God's good work here on earth. Yet it was all for show.

We lived under the same harsh religious regime that they did, although in reality they probably did much, much more on the praying front. We attended church almost daily – obscure saints days, Stations of the Cross, special Masses and three services over the weekend – and we hated it. No wonder the nuns were always so grumpy.

We dreaded Sister Consolata's return from prayers, because she was nearly always rigid with anger. Her pale Celtic face would turn crimson and she would be trying to force her black, rigid sleeves back over her podgy forearms, and her fists would be clenched. She was small and fat but sprightly, too, and she would toss her veil back, adopt the stance and then jig around her victim like Muhammad Ali.

Every night, we had to face the house meetings: that is, sessions of interrogation that could go on for hours, often through the night. They would begin innocuously, with Uncle Peter and Sister Consolata smiling benevolently as they told us how wonderful they were and how the priests and Mother Ambrose were full of praise for the way in which they ran our house.

We were never fooled by the smiles, because we knew that within seconds the meeting could turn dark and sinister. Uncle Peter and

Sister Consolata would hint that they knew something as they walked up and down the line, carefully scrutinising each of our faces to find something to give us away. It was a game for them: they would plant the seeds of guilt and then leave us standing there in our nightwear, shivering with fear and from the cold as they strolled away to the kitchen, laughing and whispering, followed by Mick Ryan* and Liam Cormac*, the two older, taller boys who were never far from Uncle Peter's side. We never knew how long they would make us stand there and we never knew what we had done, but standing in line we were tortured with feelings of such guilt that punishment was looked on as a merciful release.

All the religious stuff had the power to make me feel so awful. It made me feel as though I was unclean, that I was bad, that I deserved everything I got and more. I was tormented with guilt both night and day, and I didn't know why I felt guilty, I just did. I knew I hadn't personally nailed Jesus to the cross, and I didn't really know what sins I had committed. I knew I often had murderous and wicked thoughts, but I could wipe the slate clean of them when I went to confession. These feelings of innate guilt were being fed to us daily; every thought, every word, every deed, there was always something to feel guilty about. And each night we had to stand in the playroom in our nightwear and examine our consciences in silence as Sister Consolata and Uncle Peter walked up and down the line, searching for clues in our faces that suggested one of us might be guilty of something. Sometimes one of the little ones would break and cry and confess to something like hiding a piece of food they couldn't eat or accidentally tearing their clothes. And sometimes the nun would comfort them and praise them for being so honest and allow them to go up to bed. But other times she would lash out and punch them or kick them and use them as an example to teach the rest of us to tell the truth and confess. The game was all the more cruel because it was impossible to tell which mood she was in; she could change in a split second.

We would stand in the playroom shivering and desperately tired, often having been dragged from our beds. Sometimes it was better to confess to something, even if you had to make it up, just to end the torture.

It was not hard for us to think of sins; after all, God could see everything. I was never sure about that one, but also I wasn't sure I wanted to risk it. All sins counted, even those in your head, and they were the worst of all because you had absolutely no control over them. We would stand in line, heads bowed (because a raised chin was considered a sign of defiance), staring at the floor, as we were each ordered to examine our conscience and confess. We girls wore the long, ancient nightdresses that were given to us from the nuns' storeroom, a large basement underneath the main convent where children's clothes were laundered and recycled and dished out conveyer-belt-style to each new child or group of siblings as they arrived. And you prayed when you got sent for new clothes that one of the very few 'nice' nuns would be on duty so that you wouldn't be kitted out in dresses down to your ankles or the most hideous clothes they could find.

In truth, I very rarely did anything wrong. I didn't dare. I did my jobs the best that I could – I took pride in the shine on the floor or the whiteness of the girls' socks that I scrubbed each night by hand. I don't know why I did. It wasn't to win favour with the nun, or at least I didn't think it was, because she would always find fault and make me do whatever job it was again. Molly had to wash the boys' grey socks because she couldn't be trusted to scrub the toes and heels of the girls' socks enough to make them white again. We scrubbed the socks with cakes of hard green soap cut from a block, the same soap that we used to wash ourselves with and the same soap that we used to scrub the floors. Poor Molly never did her jobs properly. She took little or no pride in them at all, probably because she had done the jobs for so long and knew that punishments followed whether you did the jobs well or not. The nun took great pleasure in humiliating Molly and rapping her on her head with her clenched knuckles.

She didn't hit me so often, because my mum and dad used to visit, but Molly's mother was in a psychiatric hospital, and although her father lived close by, he never came to the convent. The nun used to say Molly was just like her mother, a slut and a scrubber, and that was all she would ever be. But the nun didn't know Molly as I did. Molly was kind and funny and loyal to the death and she never grassed, and I hated the nun more and more, and I hated her cruel words.

You can think up an awful lot when you are forced to concentrate. I remember being stricken with guilt over a windowsill I had forgotten to dust, or maybe a bed I had made that didn't have perfect hospital corners. I would think back over the jobs I had done before school and the jobs I had done since I'd returned, racking my brain to think of something I hadn't done properly. Sometimes if you confessed you would be praised and held up as an example to others to step forward and admit their own sins, in the hope that they would be praised too for being humble and for being honest. But it was trickery, because confessing was no guarantee of avoiding punishment. It depended on the mood of the nun and the mood of Uncle Peter, and you could never tell what their mood might be, because a kindly smile and compassionate words could easily be accompanied by a punch in the face.

The small ones, too, were punished brutally. The nun would roll up her sleeves, so they were tight and pinching, and give the children Chinese burns while they held their arms out to be hit with her wooden spoon. Their faces would be contorted with fear, waiting for the blows, but they didn't dare draw their arms away, because then they would get double the punishment.

We older ones could do nothing except watch in horror, helpless and unable to protect them. We could hide them during the day or take the blame for their mishaps, but house meetings were compulsory; everyone had to attend. Afterwards, we could cuddle them as we put them to bed, and do silly things so they would laugh and not fall asleep crying.

It was almost a relief to be dragged out of the line. It was better still if someone else was, even if it was your best friend, because it meant that you were off the hook and you could breathe a sigh of relief. But even though you were allowed to go up to bed, you still felt guilty because you would be sure there was something they would find out, or something you hadn't thought of. So you went to bed scared to fall asleep, wondering if and when you would be pulled out of your bed, listening to the raised voices downstairs, terrified in case you heard your name and then the pounding, angry footsteps of the nun as she tore along the corridor towards the dormitory to get you. Sometimes I prayed to God to protect me, but I didn't even know if he was really up there.

At one house meeting, she was so angry that she turned on Mick. We were all deeply shocked: the nun did not favour the older boys in the way that Uncle Peter did, but she never hit them – and certainly not with Uncle Peter present. Mick towered over her, standing in his usual position, arms folded, to the right of Uncle Peter. She had to jump up to punch his face, but he ducked so she missed him. Mick looked to Uncle Peter to stop her, but Uncle Peter took two steps backwards, and so did the other boy, Liam, and they just watched as Sister Consolata landed blow after blow. It was almost as though Mick felt obliged to take it, but he managed to duck a few. The rest of us tried to stifle giggles.

Uncle Peter was never as cruel to Colin and me as he was to the other kids. He would hit Molly all the time, always on the top of her head with his fist, especially when we had house meetings. The first time he went to hit me, I flinched, stepped back and looked at him with such horror and outrage that he stopped in his tracks then moved on to the next kid down the row.

A knowing look had passed between Uncle Peter and me, some kind of shared knowledge that only we two were aware of. In that fleeting moment, I think my eyes had told him 'touch me and I will kill you', or words to that effect, and for a second I felt a power over him. Of course, it was more likely to have been because our parents visited regularly and he had met my mother. That was soon after we had arrived at Tara, and what a meeting it had been.

Our first couple of years at the convent were spent in the main building, situated at the top of a hill on the outskirts of Orpington, and a long walk and bus ride from the town centre or train station. Neither our dad nor our mum drove, so visits involved long train journeys and bus rides. If we were to have a short visit either from our parents or a social worker, we would meet in the waiting room or go out for a walk around the convent or its grounds.

It was all new then, and I didn't understand the code of silence that existed. I was outraged by the violence and horrified at the way we were being treated, and I must have blabbed to Mum one Sunday afternoon while we were out walking. When we got back, we walked in through the dining room door and kids were sitting at the tables having their tea, with Uncle Peter and the nun watching over them, their arms folded in their usual sentry style. Mum barged in the door and started shouting her head off and waving her arms about in front of everyone. Everyone went dead silent and turned to look at her as she screamed at Uncle Peter, 'And you, you, I know exactly what *you* are!' The nun and Peter were trying to calm her down and steer her through the dining room towards the office upstairs. Colin ran off, but I stayed rigid, glued to the spot, shaking from head to toe, and I stayed there in silence until after Mum had gone. It was the one and only time the nun ever showed me any kindness. She pulled a chair out, picked me up, put me on her knee and spoke softly to me, and I even rested my head on her shoulder. I can't remember what she said, or even really how I felt, other than numb and very confused.

I think I must have realised then that there would be no escape, no happy ending. We were stuck there, and these strange people were all we had.

Chapter 11

Mortification of the Body Is Good for the Soul

In those early days, St Anne's Convent was an old-fashioned institution, typical of its day, and we children slept in dormitories, isolated within our own houses, away from outsiders and away from each other.

Apart from Colin and myself, Tara was made up of a motley crew of ten other kids of all ages, shapes and sizes, and we all warmed to each other straight away. There were Mick and Liam, the two oldest boys; then Molly, who was the same age as me; Patricia* and Susan*, twins about three years younger; then an assortment of little ones, including Charlie*, Simon* and Andrew*. I loved having Molly around. She was like the sister I had always wanted (instead of the horrible brother who had been put on this earth to torment me, even though he was quite funny sometimes).

Molly had been introduced to me as 'backward, thick in the head, stupid', and she kept her head down as they said those horrible things. Her hair was short and black, cut in a boy's hairstyle. The only way you could tell she was a girl was by the long, shapeless flowery dresses that she wore. I hated what the nuns said about her, and I felt so sad for her.

Molly hid her sorrow well, and she wasn't sad very often, but when she was I would try to make her laugh. Colin and I had shortened Molly's name to 'Mole', and she didn't mind at all; in fact, it made her giggle. It was great to find that she too 'had the devil in her', and through her Colin and I bonded with the others as well. We older ones (except for Mick and Liam, Peter's boys) made a kind of pact to look out for the little ones: that is, to get them out of the nun's way when she was on the warpath and to dispose of any bits of food they couldn't eat, by whatever means, usually eating it for them. Other than that, the younger kids were a pain in the arse and we would hide from them if we could so we could have a proper chat and a laugh.

Peter's boys were different entirely. They shadowed Uncle Peter constantly, falling over each other to do favours for him. They made the perfect trio: three tall, dark young men, almost always side by side. Uncle Peter stood in the middle, tall with dark, wavy hair and ugly Elvis sideburns, wearing skintight hipster bell-bottoms and a flowery shirt opened to the waist, showing all his disgusting black, curly body hair, right down to the top of his fly. On either side of him stood his younger clones, Mick to the right of him, Liam to the left. The three of them looked like an Elvis version of the Supremes. They walked the same, talked the same and stood in the same positions, looking regimental, with arms folded and legs apart, like interrogators in old war movies. Mick and Liam even adopted Peter's 'away with the fairies' poses, rubbing their chins, deep in thought, or looking up to the heavens in prayer with a gormless look that said, 'I am much too holy for this place.' There was a hierarchy in Tara, and it was immediately obvious when we first arrived.

Sister Consolata was the head of the house. That was undisputed in those early days. Uncle Peter was subservient to her, but she looked up to him for being more worldly than her, and she relished his house meetings and gazed upon him as though he were the Lord Jesus himself. I never knew if she loved him because he was so holy or whether it was because he wore very tight trousers. He was always praising her and she would go all girlish and blush. He blamed all her bad moods on us kids. He never went as far as saying, 'Oh, good punch,' but he would look at Sister Consolata after she had hit a child as if to say, 'I hope you didn't hurt your fist.' Then he would look at us as if to say, 'Now look what you made her do.' Sometimes we would feel really guilty, especially if we were trying to find the faith, and believed that it must have been our fault and would look at one another accusingly.

I think Uncle Peter was one the first examples of a radical new idea of the day: to bring in single men as father figures and role models. His commitment to religion, his background as a monk and his pious demeanour put him on par with the saints and the martyrs. For nuns, monks and priests were their pin-ups, after Val Doonican, and all of them were besotted with Uncle Peter.

Peter Rands looked and dressed like the pop stars and film stars of the time, but he was a 'man of sorrow'. He had sacrificed his life to the love of God, just as the nuns had, but he was closer to God, because when he talked he would take on a 'state of grace'. He described his physical suffering, all that whipping himself and so on, but he didn't mind it because 'mortification of the body is good for the soul'. The nuns used to fawn over him so much it was as if each and every one of them was the Virgin Mary taking Jesus down off his cross and tenderly wiping away his blood, sweat and tears with their skirts. One time, he told us how he had tied his genitals up with string and he kept the end of it in his trouser pocket so he could pull on it every now and then to cause himself agony. Mole and I could barely stifle our giggles. He always had a pained expression and the look of a martyr about him.

Uncle Peter was one of a new wave of 'assistant housefathers': that is, assistants to the nuns. I didn't hear of any other housefathers when I first arrived at St Anne's, so as far as I know he was the first. He claimed to be an ex-monk from a very strict Jesuit order, and he was pious, God-fearing and had an aura around him. Seen as and treated like a demigod from the start, Uncle Peter was pretty much given free rein to do exactly as he wanted at the convent, the church and the boys' clubs he ran. Not only did the nuns love him, but the priests loved him too.

The nuns used to look on Uncle Peter as though he was Jesus walking in our midst. 'He devotes so much time to those boys,' they would say.

'Sure, I saw that Bennett* boy coming out of there at five o'clock the other morning,' one would say, and the others would say, 'Ah, bless him, Peter's a martyr, did you ever see anyone more dedicated?' And they would all nod and agree. I was never quite sure if they weren't just having a good old gossip but in some kind of holy way.

I hated Sister Consolata, though I pretended I liked her when she was being nice – which was only when other people were around. I knew that as soon as they were out of sight or hearing range she would change back into a spiteful, evil bitch. One of her tricks was to fool us into thinking she was in a good mood, so that we would crawl around her and chat to her and laugh at her feeble, spiteful jokes. We were all so starved of attention and affection that we were willing to risk it, especially the little ones. And no matter how many times she pinched a bruise on our arms or lashed out at us with her fists, we would still draw in close to her. Words of praise or encouragement were so rare that in order to get them we would work harder, wash the most socks, clean the most rooms and work our fingers to the bone to get the shiniest floors. The only thing we would not do was grass.

To grass was considered the biggest sin in the convent by all the children. It was one of the first things, if not the very first thing, my brother and I were taught when we arrived. The other kids whispered it to us as we went off to sleep in the dormitories at night, or when there were no nuns or staff about. 'Ye never, ever tell on each other,' they used to tell us at every opportunity. And I could see the logic of this: it was a kind of 'them and us' situation, and we kids were all in it together, so we looked out for each other. We all hated the 'feckin' nuns' – Sister Consolata especially – but Uncle Peter didn't seem too bad. He had little interest in the girls. He was weird, on that we were all agreed, but the nuns' punishments were much worse, as Uncle Peter himself often reminded us.

In a way, it was like having lots of brothers and sisters. Colin and I never used to tell on each other, although, in fairness, with the pair of us it usually involved a lot of bribery. It is amazing how much you can torment a sibling when you really put your mind to it. He would get his own back on me in front of Mum, by tormenting me to the point where I wanted to kill him then acting all innocent and getting me a belt around the head.

The punishments for the girls increased as time went by. And even though Uncle Peter told us the pain should be joyous, I just never really felt that it was. One of the most gruelling tasks the nun devised was stripping the wax from highly polished floors. It was a long, painstaking and laborious task that seemed without end. For hours and hours through the night, Mole and I would scrub at the floor with worn-out pieces of Brillo Pads, the tiny splinters of wire wool embedding themselves in our water-sodden hands so they became reddened and inflamed.

I was Madam Hutton and Mole was a dirty slut who was no better than she ought to be. Sister Consolata was teaching us humility and saving us from ourselves. Uncle Peter never missed an opportunity to tell us how thankful we should be to have Sister Consolata, that she was a saint who sacrificed so much in her concern for our souls. But as much as he used to fawn over her, his interests lay elsewhere, and eventually even she began to see it. Her rage at the girls and the younger children steadily increased, but Uncle Peter's boys were mostly beyond her reach.

Apparently all of those 'called' to Holy Orders had experienced an epiphany. That is, they had seen a blinding flash of light, or they had heard the voice of God himself calling their name. For a while, I became fixated on the idea of an epiphany and I kept hoping it would happen to me, but it never did. God never spoke to me, and no archangels appeared before me, no matter how hard I prayed.

Whenever Uncle Peter would let them get a word in edgeways, the nuns loved to recall and tell us about their individual epiphanies, the special moment when they were called. I think they were each trying to outdo each other in order to impress Uncle Peter, but he just used to look bored, clasp his hands together in prayer and gaze up to the heavens until it was his turn to speak again. He liked his own stories best. As a former Jesuit monk, he was much more special than them, and he praised God every day with his pain.

I never could understand why Uncle Peter was punishing himself all the time, or why it was so important for him to punish us, too. I never felt better after being punished, and I definitely didn't feel any closer to God. I still had unholy thoughts by the bucketload, and I would lie in bed for hours thinking up ways and means to thrash, garrotte, burn and decapitate my tormentors before begging God for forgiveness, asking him to bless the bastards and turning over to go to sleep.

I knew God had much more important things to do than listen to me, but I still prayed that he would chuck a few lightning bolts at Sister Consolata's head or give Uncle Peter his ultimate high by throttling him. But there was a time, just once, when we enjoyed that wonderfully satisfying feeling of 'be careful what you wish for'.

Having been sent to bed early and deprived of *Top of the Pops* (as we often were), myself, Colin, Molly and Charlie used a small plastic effigy of a nun to vent our anger. We set up the nun's execution by balancing a ruler between the two kettles on the stove, and Colin, who was in the Scouts and knew how to do knots, made an authentic hangman's noose to swing down from the eye-level grill. By an overall majority of votes, we found her guilty as charged and placed the effigy on the ruler with the noose tied around her neck. We all volunteered to be hangman by pulling the ruler away, and after a few whispered arguments we used straws to decide. I am not sure if it was me or Molly who suggested sticking the pins in it first, but we all stabbed at the figure enthusiastically and took turns to take a peek at the real Sister Consolata as she sat in the front room, hogging the telly all to herself, to see if she reacted as we stuck the pins in. Within days, however, the nun ended up in the hospital across the road with some mystery illness. We decided that it probably wasn't a good idea to use black magic again.

I found that the holy sacrament of confession was the first bit of religion that I actually liked. As I understood it, I could basically do whatever I liked and think whatever I liked, then confess it and the slate would be wiped clean. I was very relieved to get the black magic stuff off my chest. I had read enough to know that it wasn't a good idea to be stirring up actual demons, but with confession as an option we could always come up with some new form of execution for our effigy of the nun, as long as we made sure we got ourselves absolved straight afterwards. I quite liked that and thought it would be a very good reason to believe and find the faith, because it meant I could more or less get away with murder. And those thoughts were never far away.

Chapter 12

Girls Are Not Equal

Almost from the start, it was obvious that there was a huge divide between the boys and the girls in Tara. The boys' dormitories had blue bed covers and the girls' had pink. The layout of Tara helped separate the boys and girls, too. On the left as you entered Tara from the main building was the dreaded 'playroom' – a room that is chillingly carved into the dark recesses of my mind. It was in the style of a school locker room, long and rectangular, its ancient stone floors cold and hard. At one end of the room was a row of child-sized sinks with a huge Victorian butler's sink at the head. The sinks looked out onto the school playground – St Anne's was a Catholic primary school as well as an orphanage, and the playground was at the rear of the convent. The playground led to a hill, which in turn led to a huge playing field with football goalposts and running tracks chalked out in the grass.

Staring out of the windows, scrubbing socks with the hard green soap, you could take your head to another place. In your mind, you could run across the concrete of the playground and discard your shoes as you approached the hill that led up into the field. You wouldn't need them any more – you would never need them again. And then you could hide, for hours on end, in the bushes, or in a secret bluebell vale, where no matter how carefully you trod you would always crush a bluebell. But the bluebells invited you and asked you to lie down in them and stare up into the sky. And even though you knew the nun was screaming out your name and working herself up into a frenzy, your mind saw only the beauty of the bluebells and the hypnotic, infinite world of the sky above.

Down the centre of the playroom ran a floor-to-ceiling arrangement of copper pipework, through which ran hot, sometimes scalding water, and we used these pipes to dry our washing. The pipes divided the playroom into boys on one side and girls on the other, and each side had a small bathroom, one marked 'boys' and the other marked 'girls'.

But it wasn't just about the colours of the beds in the dormitories, or the physical layout of the building, or even the obvious segregation of boys and girls for chores and homework. The divide between boys and girls went much deeper than that.

I found the atmosphere strange and creepy, and I couldn't understand that first house meeting when we had arrived where Uncle Peter had spoken and performed and the room became so quiet it was almost as if everyone but me and Colin was hypnotised by his words. The boys stayed close to Uncle Peter, forming a circle of apostles around him, hanging on to his every word – and the girls just did their best to stay out of his and the nun's way.

Molly and I were the two oldest girls in Tara and I expect they kept us there because we had older brothers. The convent had a policy of keeping siblings together, but, as much as he was able, Uncle Peter was changing the ratio of boys to girls in our house. He was selecting boys from the other houses and offering to 'take them under his wing', and the nuns were handing them over to him.

Whenever Uncle Peter appeared, he had his two minders, Mick and Liam, on either side of him. Mick was tall, muscular and tanned. He strode the halls of Tara like a twitchy ferret, always looking out for something to report, hiding around corners and listening in to conversations for something that would extend those nightly house meetings so Uncle Peter could torture us for longer with his sermons.

Liam had been a recent addition to Tara, so he was not quite so well versed in Uncle Peter's ways as Mick. Liam would sometimes keep his mouth shut. He had a younger brother, Thomas*, who had not yet been chosen by Uncle Peter to move into our house, and I wondered if some of Liam's actions were motivated by his trying to protect his brother.

I could see why the girls and the little boys always cowered in the meetings. But my mum had always taught me to hold my head up high, walk tall and look the world right in the eye. She was more of a whip-crackin', gun-totin' country-and-western gal than a peace-loving hippy.

I hated Mick at that time, because I couldn't see that he was as much a victim of the bizarre regime as we were. I rarely saw him punished physically in the way that we girls and the younger boys were, and as an older boy he was allowed privileges that we never had. It made my resentment and hatred all the greater. I could only see the predicament that we were in; I could not see or understand the survival instincts of others. We all survived as best we could, using whatever means. It often meant that we had to shut ourselves off and look away to save ourselves. It makes me so ashamed just to say that. Even now as I think of the ways in which the little ones suffered, I wish I could have helped them more.

On the occasions Uncle Peter and the nun did turn on Mick, the beatings were ferocious. Uncle Peter would trick him by going through his usual routine of berating the line of kids in front of him, making each of us wriggle on the spot as we examined our consciences like things possessed in the hope that a quick confession would allow us to go to bed. Then he would turn, like a mad thing, and start attacking Mick. Mick was not allowed to move from the spot or protect himself or hit back. We would all watch in horror as Uncle Peter would work himself up into such a frenzy that he would quite literally rip the shirt off Mick's back. Seeing the older boys being beaten was terrifying. I don't know if it was because they were so big and it looked like a grown-up beating up another grown-up who wasn't allowed to hit back.

Uncle Peter acted as though he hated the world outside the

convent, and his hatred of women was tangible: all women were whores, dirty, filthy creatures that he couldn't bear to look at. As the two oldest girls in Tara, Mole and I were made to wear dresses and skirts that almost reached the floor, but even that humiliation was not enough to satisfy Uncle Peter. He did not want us near him or his precious boys. We weren't allowed to join the other kids or our brothers in the television room without special permission, and this was rarely granted because Sister Consolata could always think up another chore to keep us occupied way into the night.

I was traumatised by the talk given to Molly and me by the nun and Uncle Peter about periods. It was excruciating, and I vowed that if it ever happened to me, I would take the secret with me to my grave. It was the Curse of Eve, apparently, for hobnobbing with a serpent. Women were cursed by God, and rightly so – Uncle Peter never missed an opportunity to spout off about how evil and disgusting women were (though not Sister Consolata, of course, who was a living saint). Women were either whores or Madonnas, nothing in between, and, apart from nuns, there were very few, if any, Madonnas. It cheered me that *the* Madonna came on the music scene to torment Uncle Peter in his final years.

Uncle Peter's talk had been creepier than anything else I had heard him come out with, and his constant references to religion were bizarre. I was still struggling to find religion or faith, so I began reading the Bible again. I hated the way it was written with all that begetting and smiting, and I couldn't understand why women were always to blame. God was a god of wrath and anger and vengeance, and my life was hell because Eve had accepted an apple.

I tried, even wanted, to accept that women were inferior and tainted because God said so, that that was how life was, but when they talked about it, it riled me up and made me feel more rebellious.

I still didn't understand religion, though I tried so hard. I wanted so much to believe in God, because I needed his help, but I never had a blinding moment, a revelation, an epiphany. All the kneeling and all the praying felt like grinding monotony. I would read the order of service, though I already knew every word by heart – 'all stand, all kneel, bow head' – as the priest droned on and on.

The nuns and priests looked strange to me in their medieval garb that set them aside from everyone else. They stood out from the crowd, exemplary, good and holy individuals whose gowns and rosaries made them worthy of respect. Parents and ordinary people would put on phoney posh voices and fawn all over them, in awe of these Sisters of Mercy, the chosen ones. The convent was known locally as the orphanage, where kindly nuns took care of the poor little orphans. Not that we mixed with the locals: well, not anyone outside of the convent, Holy Innocents' Church or St Anne's school. I expect the people of Orpington probably thought of the orphanage as a spooky old asylum at the top of the hill and that we kids were probably strange and undoubtedly bad. On the rare occasions we were seen in public, we were marched in rows, two by two.

In the 1960s in England, and probably everywhere else as well, nuns were seen as living saints, and I remember the furore when *The Sound of Music* came to the cinema screens. As one of the first portrayals of a nun as a 'woman', too, it caused quite a shock.

Sister Consolata was nothing like the nuns in *The Sound of Music*, which we were taken to see in the West End, marching two by two into coaches. I was terrified and bewildered by her maniacal rages and mood swings, and I couldn't understand why she took so much pleasure in hurting others. And she was far from the only nun to behave in that way. We all knew that not a single nun could be trusted, and it was never a good idea to stand within hitting or kicking distance of them. Sister Antonia was renowned for her kicking, and we would always run for cover when she appeared. We used to think it was funny when she was telling off a new kid, because they would duck when they thought she was about to lash out, and she would get them with a hefty kick on the shins instead, although it wasn't funny really.

Sister Consolata's bad moods often precipitated a gruelling house meeting and usually a night of punishment for Molly and me, because as girls we were usually the ones to blame. Uncle Peter would blame us for Sister Consolata's 'bad humour', as we were told to call it, and she liked that. Him crawling round her telling her that he didn't know how she put up with it gave her an excuse to carry on. She would look all saintly while he praised her, then she would praise him, and as a captive audience we had to listen to it all. Uncle Peter would put half his arse up on the table, then describe in glowing terms what a wonderful lady Constantfarta – as we called her behind her back – was and how she had made the ultimate sacrifice to Jesus. He would gaze at her in awe, gently entwining and caressing his own hands and giving her shy, affectionate smiles. And she would stand there all the while, blushing and looking all smug. When it was her turn to praise him, she would put on a gormless, flirty face with her ginger eyebrows raised to make her piggy eyes look bigger, and she would show him what great fun she was by pointing and laughing at one of us. She would defend him, too, when he was being particularly sadistic, or just downright weird.

All the Bible stuff I read said you had to be humble and not sing your own praises, so I could see why they were doing it for each other, but Molly and I found it quite sickly. I was struggling with the sin of pride at the time, and I was always in trouble for it. Sister Consolata called me Madam Hutton relentlessly now, in a nasty, mocking voice. She was determined to bring me down a few notches. She said that I 'was full of pride' and that she would 'batter it out of me, so that I had none left'. It never seemed to work. I was reading *David Copperfield* at the time and I didn't like Uriah Heep at all. I hated him pretending to be ever so 'umble, and I decided I would rather be proud and true to myself than creep around the nuns.

Chapter 13

Black and White or Colour

There was very little reading material at the convent other than Bibles or stories about saints' lives. There were no newspapers or magazines except the *People's Friend* or the *Catholic Herald*, so we had no real news about the outside world. Uncle Peter would update us on news that he considered relevant, but this mainly consisted of rants and sermons about evil women, whores who paraded around in tight hot pants and miniskirts, their disgusting faces caked in thick, cheap make-up. It was their own fault that men raped them and battered them to death. Men were innocent; they could not be held responsible for their deeds. Filthy women and their tarty clothes were to blame for everything.

The only television programmes we could count on watching were anything with Val Doonican in them. He was as big a star as Elvis in the eyes of the nuns, even though officially they were married to Jesus, which was a bit strange to my still very moral mindset. I was always looking for points to score against them, and if they were married to Jesus, what were they doing swooning over Val Doonican on a Saturday night? I felt quite self-righteous when I pointed that out to Sister Consolata.

The nun would let us sit with her when she watched Val Doonican just so that she could tell us how lovely he was and what an amazing voice he had. He used to wear hand-knitted patterned jumpers that old biddies would lovingly make for him and send him, and he would sit in a rocking chair, crooning old tunes that made you think of Ireland. Mole and I used to sit with her, not because we liked him but because it meant half an hour of no chores, and if we pretended to like the nun's programme she just might allow us to see ours.

We weren't really bothered about the lack of newspapers, or even most television programmes: all we really wanted to watch was *Top of the Pops*. That was our greatest joy, and I am ashamed to say that we would crawl around Sister Consolata and Uncle Peter in the days leading up to that magical half-hour on a Thursday evening. Try as I might, I could not get the same enthusiasm for religion as I had for *Top of the Pops*, and I rushed many a Hail Mary so I could try to catch the number one.

Not seeing *Top of the Pops* was impossible to endure. Quite often I would have to lie in bed hearing it but not being allowed to watch it – the boys were always allowed to watch it but not the girls – and I would cry myself to sleep. *Top of the Pops* was the main topic of conversation on every bus and in every playground, and crackly transistor radios were a must-have, especially small ones that you could hide. In later years, after we had moved from Tara to another house, Don Bosco, my friend Karen Bennett* and I used to sneak up to the field and lie on the grass on Sunday evenings, listening to the Top 20 countdown to the new number one. It would usually be getting dark and we would lie on our backs with the tops of our heads touching as we stared up at the moon and the stars. We would tell each other everything, and we were close enough that I could tell her to shut up when 'Kid' Jensen was doing the countdown without her getting offended, and vice versa.

We knew the words to all the songs, or at least we tried to learn them all, but with 'Maggie May' it had to be word-perfect. If no one was around, we would try to do the dances that Pan's People did and giggle because we were hopeless. I remember Karen running down Healy Drive once, ecstatic because Marvin Gaye was number one. She had managed to persuade her nun to put the 'first' Top 20 countdown on, and we already knew all the words to 'I Heard It

Through the Grapevine'. Karen was wearing hipster bell-bottoms and she had tied up the bottom of her blouse so that her waist was showing. She looked just like one of Pan's People. Her nun, Sister Rebecca*, could be kind sometimes, and she would allow Karen to buy fashionable clothes. Karen always looked beautiful, and even more so now that she had a job at the presbytery and could buy clothes herself.

I had a pair of green hipster bell-bottoms, but they didn't look the same on me. I didn't have any hips, or a bum, and they were held up with a safety pin. My mum had spent a whole day trying to find a pair small enough and adding a safety pin was the last resort. I was only allowed to wear them when she came to visit.

My reading material was restricted to whatever I could find within the cloistered walls of that ancient religious building, so I read about lots of saints and martyrs. I had discovered a bookcase in the Tara waiting room and I was able to slip the books in and out effortlessly. My dad had, of course, sneaked me and Colin a torch each when we first went into the convent; he knew what it was like to be a child having to read comics under the covers after his mum had put the lights out.

Many of the books from the waiting room bookcase graphically covered the tortured lives and deaths of martyrs with horrific illustrations that would scare the bejesus out of you. I read a book called *Rats*, which needs no summary, and chilling and gruesome short stories by Edgar Allan Poe that made my heart pound and made me pull the covers tightly over my head. Then there were books on the occult, on witches and warlocks and even evil Nazis. There were books on the concentration camps, and I numbed myself to the horror that humankind was capable of. I became desensitised to the gruesome stories from Auschwitz and I couldn't understand how people could be so evil. My dad had told me and Colin about Auschwitz, usually when he was drinking whisky. He didn't tell us the details, only stories of how his older brother had been in the war and how he and other soldiers had marched the local villagers past the gates of Auschwitz and told them that this should never, ever happen again. Dad used to get tears in his eyes as he told us, and he would say that mankind should never be allowed to forget, and that bad things happen when good people do nothing. I cried when I read about Auschwitz, and I remember the words of one poor little Jewish boy who said nothing could hurt him now, because he had already been hurt by experts. I knew how he felt.

Then I found my favourite, Charles Dickens' *A Tale of Two Cities*, and I was entranced as I read the beauty of those opening words, and I was swept into another world where the true strength of the human spirit overcomes in the end. I compared my life to those of the characters in Dickens' book, and it didn't seem so bad.

Chapter 14

And 'Thou Shalt Not' Writ Over the Door

Very soon after I arrived at the convent I had been given a 'charge'. On top of all the other daily chores that Molly and I had to do, we had to take care of a little one each. For me, it was a joy to be given a little baby to care for, and my first charge was a year-old baby called David*. He was the cutest baby I had ever seen, or maybe I just felt that way because at 12 years old I was, in effect, his little mother. Besides, in caring for him, I had extra privileges, including not having to go to the 7 a.m. Masses for obscure saints before school. I think David was the youngest child in the convent, and he needed constant care. The nuns would show minor interest in him because he was so cute, but only for a few moments. No way would they have wiped the snot off his nose or changed his dirty nappies.

Some nights he would be fretful or teething or have a cold, and he cried and cried. The nun wouldn't let me pick him up or take him to my bed, so when they put the lights out I would go and sit beside him and stroke his little head until he fell asleep.

Molly's charge was Jennifer*, who was eight years old and twice Molly's size. Molly had no interest in looking after her at all; Jennifer was a big fat lump and she got on Molly's nerves. It was funny, though, when we had a fire drill and we had to carry our charges downstairs. Molly and I used to secretly giggle about the silly rules, and we were on the floor laughing when Molly tried to carry the gigantic, sleepy Jennifer on her back. It was worth the punishment to tell the nun we were only doing as we were told.

I was trying very hard to 'get' religion at that time. I felt so much like an outsider; I just couldn't see what they could see. I would kneel by my bed every night, without laughing, and I would pray and pray that I could just 'see the light'. I would say, 'God bless Mum (and help her to behave), God bless Dad, then God bless [every family member whose name I could remember], then God bless the nuns (and forgive me for wanting them dead) and God bless Uncle Peter, the weirdo, and God bless all my friends.'

I believed in God enough to know that he could distinguish between genuine belief and asking for stuff just because you were greedy or having impure or unholy thoughts. To me, at that time, impure thoughts were hoping the fat cow nun would choke on all the cakes and biscuits she kept stuffing into her face.

I could not see their God, nor could I believe in something I could not see. I wanted to, I truly did, and I tried chanting stuff, like them, loads of Hail Marys and Our Fathers, in the hope that I would see the light, but it never happened and I envied the holy ones who found comfort in prayers and accepted the cruelty as God's will. I knew for sure Jesus used to say 'suffer little children', but I could never work out why. Little David was only one year old and he had never done anything to anyone, so I just couldn't understand why God wanted him to suffer. I and a few others resolved to protect him from the nun's uncontrollable rages, and we kids devised plans and schemes to keep him out of her way.

Kids can be pretty resourceful. We always tried to protect each other and the little ones, and we set up a series of signals to protect the baby from Sister Consolata's vicious blows. If David cried or grizzled, we would try to move him out of her range and do our best to pacify him so that his cries would not irritate her. He was teething and sometimes simply volunteering a finger for him to chew on would do the trick. On Saturdays we were given pocket money to spend at the nuns' sweet shop in the main convent, and we would try to hold some soft ones back to shove in his gob to shut him up. We could often make him giggle when we pulled funny faces, and if we couldn't lift him out of the way, behind the nun's back we would do boss-eyed faces or try to reach our noses with our tongues to make him laugh and stop screeching.

It was like a game, because the nun's moods were so unpredictable, and sometimes it was difficult to tell whether her smile was genuine or maniacal, hiding a simmering rage that would explode into her vicious little fists striking out and pounding any child that stood close to her.

Little David wasn't at the convent for very long, and although it broke my heart to see him go home, I was proud that we had kept him safe, and prouder still to show his mum how we had taught him to walk and ride his little bike.

My next charge was a little girl called Lizzie Martin*, who I was given to look after when we later moved from Tara to Don Bosco. She was a stunningly beautiful child with a big mop of black curls that framed her huge eyes and cherubic face. I would get her to repeat her name to me over and over. 'Who are you?' I would say to her, teasing and coaxing her to say her name in full in her cute lisping voice, then I would lift her up in the air and spin her around so she squealed with laughter. I desperately wanted her to know and remember who she was.

Lizzie was nearly three, and she could walk and talk, and her beaming smiles would melt even the hardest of hearts. The nuns adored her, even Sister Consolata, and they would pick her up and make a fuss of her, especially at church, when all the congregation would turn around and say 'ahh' as Sister Consolata proudly held her little hand and led her down the aisle, the rest of our house following quietly with our heads down. When we reached the altar, we each had to genuflect and make the sign of the cross before sliding into our allocated pews near the front. Sister Consolata would stay on the inside aisle seat but make me take Lizzie to the far end of the pew, near the wall, where I was to keep her quiet and sneak her out without anyone seeing if she started to play up.

We would all be in our Sunday best, with woollen hats in the winter and straw bonnets in the summer. It was the law apparently for females to wear something on their heads. I always hankered after one of the soft black-lace veils that the ladies wore, but they were for grown-ups only. The nuns loved dressing Lizzie up, and she had more clothes and coats and hats than any of us. I loved dressing Lizzie up, too; she was like a little doll and she had the sweetest nature, spontaneously giving out cuddles, just because she wanted to. I always made sure that I gently eased any knots out of her hair before the nun got her hands on her with a hairbrush or a comb and elastic bands and ribbons. The nun used hair-brushing as a form of torture for most of the girls, gleefully tugging on any knot she found until a whole clump of hair would come away in the comb. She would pull our hair back so tightly that we looked Chinese and the boys would tease us. I couldn't bear to let her touch Lizzie's hair, to treat a baby so roughly, and Mole and I would often scoop Lizzie up and hide her out of the nun's sight when tidying the girls' hair was her wicked game for the day.

Lizzie would always draw a crowd around us when we came out of church, almost the whole congregation gathering around us, cooing at how beautiful she was and telling the nuns what saints they were in taking such good care of us. Some of them would press pound notes or fivers into the nuns' hands or discreetly ask where they could make donations. The nuns loved all the attention and being thought of as saints, and they would be thrilled if Lizzie went to them with her arms outstretched to be picked up and cuddled. It made them look as though they were kind. Sister Consolata would go out of her way to ensure that Lizzie would go to her and not me, but I didn't mind, because as long as the nun was being kind to her she was safe. I should have known, of course, that it was all for show.

What followed from that was an incident that has haunted me my entire life. I had grown complacent about Lizzie's safety and genuinely believed that the nun would not hurt her.

When we moved to Don Bosco, we would take turns to keep a look out for Sister Consolata returning from the convent, where she ate her meals or attended prayers, and we could often tell by the way she was walking what sort of humour she would be in. When she was in a temper, her fat face would go bright red and she would swing her arms with her fists clenched so tightly that her knuckles turned white.

We were all given fair warning from Johnny that Sunday afternoon that the nun was heading down the hill and that she was furious. 'She looks like her head is going to explode,' he tried to whisper and shout, as he ran around warning all of us individually. I had got into the front room and was watching telly, and I was desperately trying to hang on in there until the very last moment. It was a regular routine, and we had turned it into a game, just managing to switch the television off and pretend we were working as she walked in through the back door. But I had pushed my luck too far, and as she reached the hallway Lizzie had got in her way. In a split second, she lashed out at Lizzie with a blow that lifted the toddler off her feet and brought her crashing down against the wall at the far end of the hallway.

As she stomped towards Lizzie's small, crumpled body to hit her again, I managed to stand in her way. Lizzie was conscious and whimpering and cowering in the corner, and I screamed at her to run and hide. I then stood in front of the nun, using my body as a shield. I do not know where I got the courage that day, because I am not a brave person, but I stood rigid on the spot, daring her to try to pass me. She smashed her fist into the left-hand side of my face, and I heard it crunch and could feel my cheek swelling as I reeled from the blow. Stupidly, the words 'turn the other cheek' were going over and over in my mind like a mantra, and I raised my face defiantly, only for her to smash her fist into my face again. I found religion very confusing.

Chapter 15

I Do Believe, I Do

I was so confused by religion, and no one would ever give me a straight answer. Sister Consolata said I was a heathen, and Uncle Peter said I just wasn't praying hard enough. I was invisible to the priests, because they preferred to spend their time with the altar boys.

All the teachers at school were Catholics and they didn't like being asked questions about 'faith'; they would get irritated and tell me to shut up and get on with my work. When I had briefly attended Kneller Girls' School when I was staying at the Campbell Road home, I had been blown away by Darwin's theory of evolution. The teacher had tried to answer my questions and said God making the world in seven days was a story to explain things to the simple people. She said you could believe in both things and it didn't really matter, but I couldn't see how.

Dad didn't know very much about religion either; he used to laugh and say, 'Oh don't ask me, I'm an Episcopalian,' and then double up laughing because the word was funny. He wasn't really interested in religion; it seemed to make him sad and he would try to change the subject. I thought it was because he was Scottish and they didn't seem to have much religion up there. He loved to hear about the books I was reading, though, and quite often he had read the same ones, especially P.G. Wodehouse. Colin and I shared a love of Wodehouse and so did Dad, and the three of us could talk about the books for hours and laugh our heads off when he came to visit us at the convent.

When Mum used to visit, I would try to get answers from her. She had been raised a Catholic, but she didn't have much time for it either. I remember going to church with her a couple of times, but she only went when she wanted to cadge a few bob off the priest. I don't think she had 'the faith' like other Catholics, because she used to say, 'If Mary was a fecking virgin, then so am I.'

I remember listening to passages from the Bible in church; they always threw one of them in during a service. I can't remember if it was before the long, drawn-out sermon or after, because I used to switch my ears off and drift away into another world. I found that in my head I could go anywhere I wanted and be anyone I wanted and shut out everything that was going on around me.

When I read *Jane Eyre*, in my misery I became her. I was the dull, plain, morose girl in shabby charity-school clothes who walked around with her head down and never smiled. I quite enjoyed being her, because I didn't get into trouble half so much, and I was enjoying being a martyr, too, enduring all that suffering without so much as a squeak, let alone an answer back. I thought for sure God would notice, because I was acting exactly the same way as the saints and martyrs I was reading about, and I would get my reward in heaven. I knew that they had had toenails ripped out and limbs lopped off, and I hoped that my scrubbing floors in the middle of the night wouldn't be seen as mild in comparison.

I blamed myself for not being able to understand religion. Why couldn't I see what they could see? But then I would have unholy thoughts and think about all the ones who had 'the faith' and wonder, 'What if they are just pretending?' Did they just want to make themselves look good in front of people, or even just in front of each other? I had noticed that normal people, and my mother, behaved all humble and respectful when they spoke to someone of the cloth. I used to say to Mum, 'If that priest or that nun could hear how you spoke about them behind their backs, they would excommunicate you.' I had been reading about being excommunicated, and I thought it was a terrible thing, but I was also looking into how you could go about it. I was pretty sure Mum should have been excommunicated, but I didn't go on about it too much in case it upset her.

I had been studying to do my first Holy Confession, so I was quite up on all the religious stuff at that time. Up until then, for ages, I had been merrily trotting up to the altar at every Mass and eating the body of Christ before anyone had realised that, having missed so much school, I hadn't done my first confession! That was outrageous, of course, because you had to be in a state of grace to receive Communion. The nuns were apoplectic when they realised what I had been doing, and a fast-track first confession had to be arranged. It was humiliating, as it is normally something you do aged seven or eight, and I was coming up to thirteen.

I was glad to have the one-to-one tuition, though, and the junior priest who taught me was kind and sincere and even took the time to answer my questions, albeit with a religious bias. He said lots of people couldn't see God and struggled to find faith, but it was only when you truly believed that it all became clear. I went back into Cowardly Lion mode the next time I said prayers and repeated, 'I do believe, I do believe, I do' – but nothing happened.

Chapter 16

From Tara to Don Bosco

With the new thinking of the late 1960s, there was a movement to change way that children's homes were run, which advocated placing the children or orphans in 'real' houses rather than dormitories, looked after by a mother figure (a nun) and a father figure (a random single male). So St Anne's Convent, the large gothic institution that stood at the top of the hill, was split up, with each 'family' moving into the houses that had been erected on the hill leading down from the convent to the main road. Tara, with Sister Consolata, Uncle Peter and the lay staff, moved into the second house down, Don Bosco.

The houses were purpose-built, with seven bedrooms each. There was a large bedroom for the three youngest girls, a smaller one for the two oldest (myself and Mole), a large bedroom for the three youngest boys and a smaller one shared by Colin and Philip Bennett*. The other three bedrooms were for the staff.

The top house on Healy Drive was Lisieux; the next one down was ours, Don Bosco, followed by Ancona, then by Holy Family. Each house had up to twelve kids, and siblings were usually kept together. Finally, we were able to see and spend time with those other kids who lived in the convent, whose voices we only heard occasionally when we lived in the main building and with whom we would sneak conversations when we were out in the playground.

Each 'house', that is children's home within the convent, supposedly competed to be the best. I am not sure we kids ever really fell into the spirit of that, because when we got the chance to mix we were great friends with each other. We had no need to outdo each other or show off how well behaved we were. If anything, the opposite was true. We had an affinity with each other, a shared hatred of the nuns.

It was then that Colin and I properly met the Bennett* family. They were five siblings, four of whom lived in Lisieux, right next door to Don Bosco, and I took a particular liking to them. I never knew the oldest very much. She was 15 or 16 and left soon after we moved there.

Karen Bennett was a beautiful girl with long, curly blonde hair, the face of an angel and a proper girl's figure (whereas I was straight up and down, like Olive Oyl). And I was in awe of her because her nun, Sister Rebecca, allowed her to wear miniskirts and fashionable clothes. Karen was just as beautiful on the inside as she was on the outside. Everyone adored her, me especially, and I followed her everywhere, which was probably annoying for her, because I was a year or so younger and she was a proper teenager who wore a bra! I cherished the time I spent with her; we enjoyed all the same things, books, films and radio plays, and we loved telling each other every single detail of the plots or costumes or songs.

Karen, her sister Rita and their younger brother, Hugh*, were constant visitors to Don Bosco because Uncle Peter had chosen their older brother, Philip, and moved him into our house when we lived at Tara. Philip wasn't like the other older boys. He was in a world of his own. He looked like a young Steve McQueen, the most handsome man I had ever seen and who made me feel all woozy whenever I saw his face on the screen or on a poster. Philip was really intelligent, the only kid in the convent who went to grammar school. He was quiet and sometimes wore glasses, which made him look even more handsome. He very rarely spoke to the likes of me or Molly; actually, he very rarely spoke to anyone. He was always sat at the dining room table, engrossed in books and twiddling a pencil in his hands or putting it behind his ear, then staring out of the window, then looking down again and writing something quickly. Unlike Peter's other boys, he never strutted around the place or told tales on others. He was kind and thoughtful and didn't even mind if I interrupted him to ask questions about my own homework.

The boys were allowed to sit in the dining room and do their homework uninterrupted, but it was usually only Philip in there. The girls were not allowed to do their homework until after all the chores had been done, and as Sister Consolata and Uncle Peter kept making up more and more chores for us out of spite, we never got to do our homework at all. Sometimes our work could go on well into the night, depending on what mood the nun was in. Molly wasn't bothered about her homework. She had given up trying, or maybe she just couldn't do it, because she had never had someone like my dad to sit down and show her how. Sometimes, I would go in the toilet after everyone else was asleep and scribble mine out, just so that I had something to hand in.

Molly and I were both secretly smitten with Philip, and we would help each other to do the dining room after each meal just so that we could be in his presence. It was our job to put the chairs on the tables, then brush and wash the floor, without disturbing Philip. He had a small bookcase in the room he shared with Colin, and I loved having the excuse of borrowing a book to go to his room and get Philip chatting. Philip always knew which was a good one to read, and he lent me lots of horror ones with witches and warlocks and vampires. He even had a copy of my beloved Edgar Allan Poe's short stories.

Philip didn't mind talking to me if I asked him about intelligent things, and I used to try to dream up questions during the day so I could have an excuse to talk to him. And nobody would stop me or try to drag me away, because Philip was revered and they would not have insulted him by taking away his audience.

The dynamics of the house had changed when Uncle Peter moved Philip into our house, and looking back now I think it was because Uncle Peter saw Philip as a conquest. The other 'favourites' had to take a back seat, and they didn't like it one bit. Uncle Peter bent over backwards to accommodate Philip, and for a while our lives improved.

Philip would not participate in the nightly house meetings: that is, he would stay for Uncle Peter's sermons but would walk away when the questioning and interrogating and punishing started. Uncle Peter would start to get bored when Philip left the room; he needed him there so he could show off how powerful and charismatic he was. He would follow Philip out of the playroom and try to persuade him to come back. Sister Consolata used to get agitated at this, and although she would carry on with the rituals with just the other boys backing her up, we could see that she was becoming more and more irritated and that she just wanted to get away and follow Uncle Peter. She was jealous of Philip to the point of fury, but she didn't dare let it show. Until Philip moved in, she had been the focus of Uncle Peter's attention; she was the boss and he had had to ingratiate himself with her. Her power had shifted, and she had only the girls and the little ones to take it out on.

When we moved into Don Bosco, Sister Consolata and Uncle Peter remained as housefather and housemother, but the care and control of the house passed to Uncle Peter. He lived and slept in Don Bosco and had the biggest staff bedroom in the house, while the nun still ate and slept and prayed in the main convent building. Her temper grew worse as Uncle Peter usurped her, but there was little she could do, as she was tied by her duties as a nun to the main convent up on the top of the hill.

With full control of Don Bosco, Uncle Peter moved a friend in to live with us. Uncle Jimmy was a former monk, like Uncle Peter, and they were really good friends, because Uncle Peter allowed Uncle Jimmy to share his bedroom, even though there was an empty staff bedroom going spare. Uncle Jimmy was tall with a full head of long, light-brown curls, like the stars on *Top of the Pops*. He liked his curls, because he often used to walk around the house with rollers in, wearing a flowery housecoat. He never used to speak to us; in fact, he treated us as though we were rats underneath his feet. We all hated him – at least the girls, the younger kids and Colin did – and we would laugh about him behind his back, because he looked so funny in his curlers and the things he used to wear. I think Sister Consolata hated him, too, because Uncle Peter started to spend more time with Jimmy than with her, and it would make her angry. Uncle Jimmy was his new favourite, and even Philip got pushed aside.

Uncle Peter thought very highly of Jimmy indeed, and so did the older boys. They would all go up to Uncle Peter's bedroom for hours, or go on outings to London or to the pictures. The girls were never allowed to go on those outings or have any privileges, because we were usually being punished, and so too was Colin. For some reason, although he was one of the older boys too, Colin wasn't part of their group. He had to go to bed early, like the girls, and he was never allowed to join the older boys when they went out.

Colin couldn't hide his hatred of Uncle Jimmy and never even made any attempt to. Jimmy was rude and aggressive; he despised the girls and the younger kids and would simply push us out of his way if he wanted to get past, seeing us as unworthy of any words such as 'excuse me' or 'do you mind'. One evening in the kitchen he pushed Colin out of the way, but Colin must have been angry or something because he said, 'Fuck off, you big poof,' and Jimmy hit him, knocking him onto the ground. I saw what happened and started to scream, but Jimmy pushed me out of the kitchen door and carried on kicking Colin as he lay on the ground. Within seconds, Uncle Peter had run into the kitchen, too, and he slammed the dining room hatch shut because I was trying to crawl through it. I could hear the two grown men punching and kicking Colin as if he were a sack lying on the floor. As I tried to get into the kitchen from the back door, Mick Ryan pulled me away and covered my mouth so no one could hear me.

When Peter and Jimmy had finished, they finally allowed me into the kitchen, where I found Colin lying in a blood-spattered mess on the floor. I felt completely powerless as I knelt beside him, begging him to speak to me, to tell me he was all right. I lay next to Colin crying. I didn't know what else to do.

Philip came to our rescue. He helped me get Colin up the stairs to his bed, and both of us spent the night sitting over him in vigil, gently dabbing Colin's poor swollen face with wet flannels and getting him anything he needed.

Sister Consolata became angrier and more cruel as time went by, and I even heard her arguing with Uncle Peter on the landing one night. For some reason, she had moved out of the main convent and was now sleeping in a formerly empty staff bedroom in Don Bosco. I heard the raised voices and made out I needed the toilet so I could go and take a look. 'It's not right!' I heard the nun yell, and Uncle Peter was telling her to keep her voice down. I noticed Uncle Peter's bedroom door was open and Jimmy was sitting on his bed.

I didn't really know what it was about, and I was in a hurry to get back to my room and tell Molly that I had seen the nun without her veil! She looked just as horrible as we had imagined – in fact, worse! She had short, bright-ginger hair, combed back like a man's, and it looked as though it was covered in Brylcreem. Her face was ugly, as we knew it would be, with rolls of fat unrestrained by her white mask and bib. And her face was bright red, of course, because she was in a fuming temper.

The arguments between the nun and Uncle Peter became more frequent after Jimmy moved in, but she couldn't win. It seemed as though Uncle Peter was now the undisputed boss.

His sermons became even more anti-women, as he laid the blame for all life's ills fairly and squarely at the hemline of the miniskirt. 'How many innocent young boys' lives will be ruined by this blasphemy?' he yelled, and then he would look accusingly at Molly and me, whose ancient hand-me-down dresses hovered approximately two inches above our ankle socks.

Like Philip, Uncle Jimmy had little interest in the house meetings. He would stay for the beginning, but Jimmy would get bored and wander off and Uncle Peter would follow him, leaving Sister Consolata angry and frustrated. We kids were relieved to have the interrogations shortened, but rather than letting us off the hook, the nun would make us say nightly prayers instead, kneeling on the hard floor of the house waiting room. The visitors' waiting room was the most formal room in the house, and kids were not allowed in there without special permission. It had the statutory bloodied crucifix up on the wall for visitors to stare at, and it had replaced the playroom as the room that was now used for the nightly house meetings and interrogations.

When the meetings came to an abrupt end and her fun was spoiled, she would make us all kneel, look up at the bloodied crucifix and chant the rosary. During the 40 days of Lent, the rosary was replaced by the Stations of the Cross, or the Via Dolorosa, the way of pain, the 14 Stations (or stops) where Jesus had fallen on his route to Calvary carrying the cross, on the way to be crucified. The Stations are usually placed around the walls of a church, and you turn and pray at each Station, remembering the pain and suffering our saviour endured. The most exciting part of it is shuffling one, or possibly two, steps to the right or left. As much fun as they were, we hated them when we had to do them three times a day, once in church at 7 a.m., then again at school and once more just before we went to bed.

It didn't make me love Jesus, or feel anything for his suffering. I just wanted to hurry up and get to the one where he was laid in his tomb, so I could catch the number-one record on *Top of the Pops* or read the next bit of my book under the covers. I just didn't get it, and I would open my eyes and look around the church or the school just to see who else's eyes were open and who else didn't get it. The story was almost 2,000 years old; it wasn't like it had happened the day before, or was real, like the Aberfan Disaster.

At the convent, I had grown desensitised to physical cruelty, to the nails they hammered into the hands of Jesus or the spear they stabbed into his side. It was horrible and gory, and as a child I had always buried my head under my dad's arm to avoid looking at blood and guts when we were watching a film on the telly. In those days, I could feel the pain of others in the same way as my dad and, like him, I couldn't bear to see anyone being hurt. Dad understood my tears and felt my pain, and he would suck the air in through his teeth and say, 'Oh, jeesy peeps, ooh, ooh, ooh,' if I cut my finger or grazed my knee, and he would rush to dab the injury with antiseptic and put a plaster on it. I never used to bother making a fuss if it was only Mum at home, because she would just belt me round the ear and tell me to stop whingeing.

Chapter 17
Better the Devil You Know

....

There weren't any announcements or fond farewells; we just came home from school one day and Uncle Peter was gone, and he had taken Jimmy with him. The convent was buzzing with gossip, at least it was among the adults – nobody would tell us anything.

Sister Consolata had a new friend now: Mrs Munro*, the 'cleaner' at Tara, who had come with us to Don Bosco. They had always been close, at least close enough that Mrs Munro never had to do any actual cleaning. And they had become closer still, as Uncle Peter had spent more and more time with Jimmy and the boys.

Mrs Munro was a typical hard-working middle-aged woman who had been around long enough to get paid for the cleaning, but also to get the convent kids to do it for her. She had dedicated her working hours to sucking up to the nun and Uncle Peter, so much so that she became known as an 'absolute saint' throughout the community. She loved people to talk about what a hard-working woman she was, and she used to sit at the kitchen table for hours on end, telling the nun how hard she worked while they drank coffee and ate biscuits.

At one time, the saintly Mrs Munro gifted us kids in Don Bosco a couple of rabbits as pets, and she got her husband to build the rabbit hutches. Everyone was, of course, informed of her generosity and kindness, and I think it got a mention in the Sunday Mass weekly news. Such are rabbits, pretty soon two became four, four became eight and so on, and our rabbit population increased dramatically. We kids loved all the rabbits and petted them and named them as each new batch of baby bunnies arrived.

All kids love their pets and become attached to them, but for us they were so much more. We cared for them as if they were precious jewels, even arguing over who got to clean the cages. We would rush home from school to see them and we were supposed to take turns to feed them, but we all wanted a go so they grew very fat.

We were still basking in the joy of Uncle Peter and Jimmy going, but our joy was to be short-lived. Uncle Peter had warned that there were others out there far worse than him. Obviously, he wasn't lying, because our next experimental uncle was a psychopathic sadist and we began to wonder if Uncle Peter had perhaps been a saint after all. If we had thought life hard before, with the arrival of Uncle Tim (or Bimbo, as we came to call him) it was about to become a hundred times worse. He was about to stamp his own particular brand of cruelty on his new reign in a way that none of us would ever forget.

Uncle Tim was a small weasel of a man with a Napoleon complex, and we children thought he would have been far happier if the job had come with some sort of formal, prison guard-style uniform. I remembered seeing a Norman Wisdom film where Norman kept trying to get a job in the police, but he kept being turned away because he was too small. I asked Uncle Tim once if that was his problem, and although I went to bed without dinner it was totally worth it.

Where Uncle Peter would carry out his inspections with his arms folded in front of him, Uncle Tim was more casual and would walk slowly behind the nun with his hands clasped behind him, à la Prince Philip walking behind the Queen as she inspects her troops. Of course, Bimbo's army was a sick, imaginary one in his head. We kids were getting older when he arrived on the scene, and we had been through much. With the departure of Uncle Peter and fewer visits from the nun (the nuns were gradually being moved back to the main building as lay staff took over the care of the homes, but as the transition was taking place they still slept in our houses), we were getting bolder and more rebellious.

Like a goose-stepping Nazi general, Uncle Tim saw us kids as society's waste, children that he could use to satisfy his mad craving for power and control. Unfortunately for him, his crazy little scheme to take over a tiny empire of his own was flawed, because he was faced with a little army of renegades who had just about had enough.

I remember how his face lit up soon after he arrived when he saw the nun punch a child. It was as if he had been given the green light. We despised Bimbo for his physical cruelty and we had no respect for him whatsoever. It became a vicious battle, and we would hit him where it hurt: his lack of height and his receding hairline. 'Did you know that Alan Ladd stood on boxes, so he would be the same height as his leading lady?' someone would say as we sat down to dinner. Then we would all have a full-scale conversation about different things they could have done, like make the actress stand in a hole. The conversation would deteriorate from then on until we were all crying with laughter. Bimbo would go rigid and white with rage, unable to do anything because the nun would be looking on. He rarely hit us when the nun was present; he usually waited for her to go up to the main building before he really got started. However, when no one was looking I suffered his sly punches to the kidneys, which he found so hilariously funny. He was cruel, and his face lit up like he was a mad axeman when Sister Consolata gave him the go-ahead to slaughter all of our pet rabbits for dinner.

The adults – Sister Consolata, Bimbo and Mrs Munro – would spend most of their time in the kitchen, talking and drinking coffee. I don't know whose idea it was, but the three of them were in full agreement. They had decided that our pet rabbits should be killed so we could eat them. And so we who loved them watched in horror as Mrs Munro and Bimbo demonstrated to the older boys the quickest way to kill a rabbit. They each took turns pulling a screeching Snowy or Fluffy from their hutches, hanging them upside down, then gleefully copying Bimbo's perfect rabbit punch to the back of the head. But the boys' blows weren't perfect, and the poor creatures squirmed and died in agony, their poor eyes bulging from their heads. Then Mrs Munro demonstrated how to disembowel, skin and dismember them. I don't know how long it was before I turned away.

It is so hard now to describe the horror, and I feel shame that I did not stop the slaughter, or at least get the little ones out of the way. Maybe I did, maybe I tried to. I honestly do not remember. Maybe some primeval part of me made me stand there and watch, like the Romans watched the gladiators in the arena. I remember vomiting.

Yet the vile and cruel debacle was far from at an end. Sister Consolata revelled in making rabbit stew and rabbit pie out of our beloved pets and serving them to us for our evening meal. The horror was brought to an end by Aunty Molly, a kindly lay member of staff. Aunty Molly was a ray of sunshine in our lives. An elderly lady who lived on the estate next to us, she would come in for a couple of hours a day to help with teatime and the washing and ironing. She could never challenge the nun directly, but we could tell she was on our side by the little things she did. One Christmas, Mole and I were mortified to be given 'ginger tights', a horrible shade of orange, in our presents, and we swore we would never wear them. Aunt Molly boiled them in a saucepan with washing powder until they turned the right shade for us. She would also find ways of helping us avoid hidings, by making light of whatever we had or hadn't done, or by distracting the nun by waving coffee and a chocolate biscuit under her nose. She was bottom of the rung authority-wise, but on the day of the rabbit slaughter she started clearing away the crying kids' full plates right under the nun's nose and gave her a look that could have killed her dead on the spot.

I hated Bimbo with a vengeance, but not half as much as he hated me, especially after I had brought a mother into the room where he was abusing her son. He would never forgive me for that.

I had answered the door to a parent one Sunday afternoon and led her directly to the dining room, not to the official waiting room. Parental visits were quite formal in that they always took place in the waiting room. There was no question of the parents seeing any other parts of the house. The same applied to social workers: they, too, never saw our actual 'living quarters'. The dormitories, bedrooms, playrooms and so on were scrupulously clean and highly polished, as mine and Molly's scullery maids' hands showed, but they were never seen by anyone outside of the home.

That Sunday afternoon, Charlie, a five-year-old boy with a doting mother, was still sitting at the dining table with all the chairs stacked up around him as Molly and I swept and washed the floor. We had had cheese salad for Sunday tea, and Charlie couldn't bear the taste of cheese in any way, shape or form. Colin, Mole or I would always try to sit next to him for meals, so that we could get rid of it off the plate by eating it for him. On that day, though, he was still sitting at the table, breaking his little heart that the cheese was making him heave, as Uncle Tim balanced a long-handled broom over his head, crashing it down onto him every time he spat the cheese out. Uncle Tim relished forcing vomit back into the mouths of children who could not eat what he had cooked. When the doorbell rang, I felt as though God had finally answered my prayers as I opened the front door to Charlie's mother, who had arrived unexpectedly, and I led her directly into the dining room, where her son was being punished.

Naturally, all hell broke loose, and the nun came running from the television room, screaming with her fists waving about. She managed to catch me with a few blows as I ran for the stairs, but she was too bothered by what was happening in the dining room to kill me.

After Charlie's mother left, an urgent house meeting was called, and all the staff had to attend, too. Sister Consolata spent ages marching up and down the row of kids, telling everyone how awful I was and that because of me they would *all* have their privileges stopped for a week. 'And you, Madam Hutton,' she kept saying, her

Colin and me: the whole of Virginia Water was our playground, and even the stones on the ground were our toys.

Scenes from around Virginia Water,
including Holloway Sanatorium.

Myself and Colin playing in the grounds of the nurses' home.

Making mud pies and daisy chains in 1962.

Me with my childhood friend Ray.

Me on my bike outside Bramdene.

I knew I had been a happy child before the convent
– and I had the pictures to prove it.

My mother as a young woman.

Me in my Cathy McGowan trouser suit.

Karen's birthday, Lisieux, 1969: the only photo I have from the convent.
I am sitting on the far table looking back towards the camera.

Me in 1974 (second from right), aged 17, with Big Lynn (far left) and two other friends.

With my dad on my wedding day.

Reunited with Mum.

On holiday in Egypt, June 2000: Mum, me and my son Jak. The photo was taken by my dad.

Graduation day with my lecturers: Neil Nixon in his Masters garb, Pauline Hall and Mike Ellis

With my dad, my brother and my two sons at my graduation.

arms folded tight with anger, her gnarled little fists popping out every now and then to hammer the point home on my head. I didn't dare answer back: it was the angriest I had ever seen her, and I still thought she was going to pulverise me. 'No one is to speak to you for three months,' she said. I had 'shown Don Bosco up', I had 'stuck my big nose in where it wasn't wanted' and I had 'betrayed the Don Bosco family' – so no one was allowed to speak to me. And that was it, Sister Consolata had made her decision: none of the kids, none of the staff and, of course, none of the nuns could speak to me. I half felt like laughing, because I thought, 'Is that the best you can come up with?' But I didn't dare say it.

I wasn't bothered anyway; I didn't want to talk to any of them, I hated the lot of them. The not-talking lasted for a few days, but then the kids and staff used to talk to me when the nun wasn't looking, and Colin and Molly used to make faces at me behind her back. But by then I had discovered the Brontës and my mind was away in a whole new world. My 'becoming Jane Eyre' coincided with my summer of silence and being sent to Coventry. We were coming up to the long summer holidays, and I had lost all interest in playing with the other kids, or even chattering to anyone who would listen, as I delved deeper and deeper into the books I had found in the waiting room.

I relished my solitude, and while the others played flying angels on a death-defying maypole with ropes hanging down, I would curl up under a tree with a book, too impatient to find out what happened over the page to care what went on in the world around me. I was managing to read a book a day, sometimes two if I could keep my eyes open long enough as I read with a torch under the bedcovers. I read everything I could find, and if I couldn't find anything new, I would reread old favourites. To this day, Wodehouse's *Uncle Dynamite* stays close to my bedside table.

To Bimbo, we were scum and not even worthy of his breath, so he devised a system where he didn't have to speak. For example, if you were sitting in a chair and he wanted it, he would click his fingers, which meant 'move'. If he had to click his fingers twice, he got really angry. I could do nothing to hide my pure hatred of the man. It was as if he got some sick form of pleasure from the physical punishments he inflicted on the children in his care. I had seen him tormenting and torturing the little ones, and I had witnessed him pushing Mole down the stairs when he thought she had been looking in his room.

I was 14 when I suffered my worst physical attack at St Anne's, and it came, of course, from Uncle Tim, who hadn't forgotten how I had exposed him in front of a parent. I had been sitting in one of the more comfortable chairs in the television room, relaxed and excited that *Top of the Pops* was coming on. Sister Consolata had gone up to the main convent for prayers, and she wasn't expected back that night. It was as if Bimbo had planned his next move, his moment for revenge, step by step. When he clicked his fingers to tell me to move, I told him to 'fuck off'. I knew he would attack me – he knew the rules as well as I did, and he knew I would have no excuse for my behaviour; defying staff was a major rule violation at St Anne's – but I didn't care. I had made up my mind never to be demeaned by him again. I knew what was coming.

His first punch to my face was spot on. My head flew back, and I was stunned as the next blows rained down onto my face and body. At one point, he used my hair to pull my limp body from the chair, and I felt it being ripped from the roots as he hurled me to the ground. I could hear the voices of Mole and Colin screaming, and Colin jumped on his back, trying to pull him off me. Then the nun, who had returned unexpectedly, joined Bimbo's tag team and punches were flying everywhere.

Of course, Colin and I didn't win – we couldn't – and to make matters much worse, Mum turned up out of the blue soon after and saw the injuries to my face. She looked straight at Bimbo; she knew that he had done it. She flew at him, grabbed him by the throat and smashed him back against the wall. The nun was trying to pull her away and in the kerfuffle got a whack on the jaw, which I was pleased about. Eventually, they calmed Mum down enough for all of them to go off and talk in the office. I don't remember anything after that, only Colin and I standing in Mother Ambrose's office later while she told us what terrible children we were to bring such disgrace on the wonderful name of St Anne's. As I expected, the nuns took Uncle Tim's side, and I was in the worst trouble I had ever been in. To make it worse, my mother had also, along with Colin and myself, assaulted a nun and a member of staff. I was overwhelmed with guilt.

Still, I was proud of our fightback, and I couldn't wait to tell all my friends at school. I was even proud of my black eye. 'We showed them, didn't we, Col?' I said as I chased after him up the hill towards the wrath of the Mother Superior. Colin just told me to shut up and leave him alone, he didn't want to speak to me, not ever.

Our accusers were waiting in the office when we arrived. Sister Consolata and Bimbo were looking truly shocked; the nun especially looked particularly holy and humble. They could not imagine what on earth had possessed Linda and Colin to attack them.

'Have you got anything to say for yourselves?' Mother Ambrose demanded, but the only answer she really wanted to hear was the word 'sorry'. Blame had already been established: she had heard about me and how bold I was several times already. 'You think you are getting away with things, but you are not!' she screeched at me. Her voice kept fading away, like Richard Harris's when he played Cromwell, to a high-pitched squeak, which showed just how angry and emotional she was about the incident. She was sick, probably dying, and Colin and I had made her so angry that she was struggling for breath. Sister Consolata and Bimbo glared at me and Colin as though we were probably guilty of causing her consumption, too.

Colin said sorry almost straight away, but I hesitated for a few minutes. It just wasn't fair. I didn't want to say sorry because I wasn't sorry; I wouldn't mean it even if I said it. I knew I had to say it, though, because otherwise we would never have got out of there, but when I did I tried to make it sound like I was saying it begrudgingly.

We lost all our privileges for a month, which meant no parents visiting, no television, no days out, no pocket money. In addition, everyone was to carry on with Sister Consolata's previous punishment: I was to be ignored by all; there was to be no conversation with me whatsoever.

'That wasn't so bad,' I said. I tried to cheer Colin up about all the punishments we faced as we walked back down the hill. I was used to them, and I thought he was too, but he was angry. He looked as though he hated me.

'You just don't get it, do you?' he yelled at me, and I could see tears in his eyes. 'Every time you get in trouble, I get in trouble too. You're just like Mum!'

I was mortified by what Colin had said. I wanted him to like me again; I needed him. We were supposed to be on the same side. I didn't care what the nuns did – they couldn't hurt us any more – but I cared what Colin thought, and I wished that I could have turned the clock back and kept my big mouth shut.

Chapter 18
Why Didn't We Tell?

Colin and I liked Miss Bradshaw. Omni had established that. So why hadn't we told her what was happening at the convent? We had visits from both our parents, yet we hadn't told them the whole story either. Why?

It was a question that I didn't know the answer to. Why didn't we tell? I had asked myself that question hundreds of times, and there in the witness box I couldn't think of an answer, not one that made any sense, not one that would be accepted in a court of law. I stared down at the papers in front of me, taking my time to answer Omni's question. Why hadn't I spoken up at the time? Why had I waited more than 30 years to come forward?

I flicked through the reports given by Sister Consolata and Peter Rands: 'Linda has become arrogant, Linda has become sulky, Linda has become stubborn.'

'I felt something was wrong. I found the opportunity to speak to her on her own,' Miss Bradshaw had written in her reports, giving a minute-by-minute breakdown of one of her visits to us. She had gone on to say, 'Linda tells me she is fine,' and then she said I had changed the subject.

I don't know why I didn't tell Miss Bradshaw the truth. I don't know why I felt the need to change the subject. I suppose I knew that if I said anything, my life would become a hundred times worse. Telling tales was the biggest sin and usually resulted in extreme punishments for being such a terrible liar, saying such wicked things about the saintly nuns. No one would have believed me, not even Miss Bradshaw.

I remembered that withdrawing into myself, burying my head in a book and so on, had been seen as signs of my 'stubborn defiance'. Instead of allowing me to keep out of the firing line, it often led to more interrogations and more beatings, because the nun had set her heart on breaking me. I can't say that my 'withdrawal' and failure to speak were due to fear or respect or whatever the hell it was those weirdos wanted from me. The truth is, it probably *was* stubborn defiance. I had long ago given up trying to reason with the nun or trying to use words to calm fraught and traumatic situations. Words meant nothing to Sister Consolata. Words were lies. Fists were real.

I remembered the terror of the nightly interrogation; I remembered it being my turn to be the 'guilty one', the cause of everyone else's suffering. All fingers were pointing at me. I had no idea what I had done that attracted so much hate, so much anger, so much rage. I was physically pulled out of the line, and I trembled in fear. I had seen it done to others so many times. The memory of being pulled out of the line for the first time was still with me, and standing there in the witness box I was reliving every moment of it. This is what happens if you tell.

'Admit it. Admit it!' In my mind's eye, I could see the rage-filled face of Sister Consolata and I could feel the pounding of her fists on my head and on my body. I flinched and cowered.

I had done the drying-up that evening, and there were more than enough witnesses to that effect. Therefore, without any doubt or need for further evidence, they had caught me. I had put the cups away in the cupboard upside down. Even after the nun spent several hours trying to beat it into me, I did not understand what was so wrong with upside down – and to this day, I still don't. In fact, even now I cannot put cups away without a shiver running down my spine, but I have learned to put them in the cupboard however I want. I just keep my fingers crossed that the crockery police haven't got me under surveillance.

There was no reasoning with the nun; there was no connection on a human level whatsoever. To her, we were just another part of the horrible life she had chosen. I accepted that I couldn't win, I couldn't beat the system. I was powerless, helpless; I couldn't protect myself, let alone anyone else. I remember so clearly how I felt at the time. I went to bed crying, having sworn that nothing, but nothing, would make me cry. I had been beaten both physically and mentally. I was utterly defeated and had absolutely nothing left to fight with other than my thoughts of revenge, my thoughts that one day I would tell my story. Maybe the nun could see the knowing look in my eye, and maybe she had read my behaviour as defiant. Maybe she was right.

The reports of Miss Bradshaw were quite accurate, albeit, I thought, slightly euphemistic. Just how deep had Miss Bradshaw delved? Probably not far – it wasn't the done thing in those days. Omni didn't refer to any of the negative reports, only the ones where social services had referred to us as fine. Omni acted for the defendants and he showed that they had done their duty.

Things were far from fine, that I remember clearly, and the papers in front of me brought all those memories flooding back. They related to my summer of silence, the memories of which are as clear to me now as they were then. I had seen my brother beaten to a pulp. I had been beaten to a pulp myself. I had seen horrendous abuses of other children, yet Colin and I had said nothing. In fact, none of us ever did. The convent children's pact of silence went beyond the usual childhood code of kids not grassing on each other. In our case, bizarrely, it included not grassing on the nuns or staff either.

It seems incomprehensible now, as an adult, to see how such a large number of people, children and adults alike, could be brainwashed or subjugated to such an extent that no one ever said anything. For us kids, the repercussions of grassing simply weren't worth the risk. No one would ever believe a kid over a nun.

But it was more than fear of punishment that kept our secrets; it was a kind of indoctrination. At our house meetings every night, Uncle Peter had reinforced our pride in Tara, later in Don Bosco. He would remind us how privileged we were to be in 'his' house. We were the flagship of the convent, he would tell us, and all the other kids in the other houses would give anything to move into our house.

We didn't often see the kids from the other houses, except when we were in church. Each house would get paraded along in our Sunday best for every church service. On a Saturday evening it was Novena, then eight o'clock Mass on Sunday morning and Benediction at four o'clock on Sunday afternoons. That was apart from saints' days, when we were allowed to go to the 7 a.m. Mass, in our school uniforms so we could go straight on to school after.

Going to church didn't make me feel holy – I still had all the same thoughts going on in my head as I did when I was in the playground or going off to sleep. In fact, I had them even more – anything to take my mind off the dull, dreary surroundings and the droning voice of the priest trying (but failing) to sound songlike as he said the same boring words day after day, week in and week out, so people wouldn't drop off to sleep. It didn't used to work, though. The older people and a lot of the nuns used to keep their eyes closed so they would look holy, but I always thought they were nodding off, because sometimes they looked startled when we all had to stand up or kneel down.

We children weren't allowed to keep our eyes closed, because one of them would be sure to be watching us and would batter us if we did, and if we weren't in a nun's line of vision the priest could see us, and so could God. I wasn't bothered about the priests, because they would go off into a trance when they were holding the Mass. From the minute they stepped up to the altar in their flowing robes and finery, they would get a faraway look in their eyes and would start speaking to the congregation like a kindly but stern shepherd rounding up his sheep. I never used to listen to anything any of them had to say, because their boring voices merged all their boring words together and I was sick of stories about shepherds and sheep.

I liked to look around the church, though, and stare at the strange, grotesque statues and pictures and stained-glass windows. I was drawn to them; they fascinated me yet repelled me. Holy Innocents' Church was huge, and staring up into the huge rafters and looking around at the creepy artefacts could keep me occupied for ages. I had no watch and there was no clock on the wall, but I timed the services by the rituals. As soon as you heard that little bell tinkle, you knew the service was coming to an end and you could have some breakfast! You all had to kneel and bow when the priest held the body of Christ in the form of a dry wafer up to the heavens and the altar boys let loose with the incense. You weren't meant to look up at that bit, but I always did because I was always hoping to see a ray of light or something.

There were very strict rules on how we were to behave in church, and not one of us, not even the bolder ones, would dare to do anything to bring the nun's wrath down upon us. We all had to look especially smart for church, and the nun would take great pleasure in yanking the girls' hair into pigtails using harsh elastic bands that would pull individual hairs out by the root and stay tight long enough so you couldn't smirk in church. You weren't allowed to speak or cough in church either, not even if you had a cold. I remember when one of the little ones had a cold and she had to sit in the front row with Sister Consolata in the row behind her in case she dared to cough or sneeze. The child's name was Katy* and she was about six years old. Katy was a very nervous little girl, with short, badly cut hair and round National Health Service glasses. She always stood knock-kneed with her hands twisted together. I think she had been in the convent for a long time. Poor Katy was choking throughout the service with Sister Consolata screwing her fist into her back every time she spluttered. I was in the same row as the nun and watched in horror as she tormented the child throughout the Mass, Katy's face growing redder and redder as she struggled not to make a noise. I went back to the make-believe world inside my head.

Church was a good place to think and to ponder, and in a weird way I liked the silence. Everyone had to keep to the rules, because the open space and the stone walls captured and echoed every single solitary sound, and the statues looked down on you accusingly. I think you were supposed to think about God and stuff like that, and I did try, but I could never really accept it all as real, and I wondered what it had to do with my life. I knew the Bible stories inside out and upside down, but I just didn't think they were that good any more. I had read much better stuff.

I had grown accustomed to the cruelty, the chores and the constant beatings: they were the dark, creepy secrets of the home that I lived in, too horrible to discuss with any outsider. Convent kids were closer than most. Like battered siblings, we shared those awful secrets only between ourselves, too ashamed for anyone to find out the truth.

Chapter 19

The Girl I Used to Be

When the trial adjourned for the first day, Lynn and I returned to our hotel room. I had been confronted with a childhood background that fully justified all my pills, therapists, odd behaviour and excessive love of bottles of vino, and I felt like I was being torn apart, as if I didn't know what the truth was any more. I began to question my own sanity. Without the guidance of those I love, I have little or no faith in my own judgement. I try to make out that I am really clever, but inside I feel like a phoney. Fortunately, or unfortunately, for me, the only spiritual and emotional support I had to hand was my lobotomised best friend who swore a lot. Yet without her company I doubt I could have gone through with it all.

Too exhausted to go out to eat, Lynn and I lay on our hotel beds and chatted about the events of the day, dissecting each party's point-scoring and wondering what the judge thought. His face was giving nothing away. I still couldn't speak to my solicitor or barrister, or even my psychologist at a time when I needed a psychologist the most. I wasn't allowed to discuss the trial with them until I had finished giving my evidence and the judge released me. Lynn and I chatted for most of the night, our brains too hyperactive to sleep even after we had taken some Nytol. Happily, most of our conversations ended in laughter. We always managed to take sensible discussion to the level of the absurd.

I had brought everything bar the kitchen sink up to Leeds with me, including hundreds of childhood photos. I needed to look through them, I needed to remember. I felt as though Omni had tried to destroy every single happy memory I had ever had. He was portraying my beloved father as feckless, irresponsible, even negligent, when I knew in my heart that my dad had done everything he possibly could. The 1960s were a long time ago. Fathers didn't get custody of kids then, and help with housing and finances was minimal or non-existent.

The photographs made me laugh: I always had a dirty face, an uppity attitude and a disastrous haircut. The happy, funny memories came flooding back. I desperately needed those memories to cushion the horror of the court proceedings that were going on around me. As I flicked through the photo albums and held the negatives up to the light, I began to recognise that kid in the photos. She wasn't the sobbing, blubbering old lady who had stood in the dock today; she was full of life, full of mischief, full of joy. I remembered my cheeky self, the cocky, streetwise little urchin who was afraid of nuffink and nobody. I needed to remember the kid I used to be. I needed to reawaken her, bring her back. I needed her to face the next day's proceedings. I needed her to face Omni.

As I drifted off to sleep, I thought about Virginia Water, a pretty village in Surrey that was the first family home that I could remember clearly. We lived there before Colin and I started school, and the whole of Virginia Water was our playground. And there I was sitting in the hairdresser's chair. They had placed a board across the chair for me to sit on, so the hairdresser could comb and cut my hair. I smiled inwardly as I remembered the grumpy face that had stared back at me from the mirror. My bottom lip was almost touching the floor. I didn't care about having my hair cut, but I was wearing nothing but an adult T-shirt and I was soaked to the skin! 'Now you will sit still or I'll beat the daylights out of you,' my mum said as she shook her fist at me. Actually, everyone was soaked – I had put up quite a fight. I could see Mum was laughing really, and so were a couple of the other ladies, but I could overhear a couple of women in the corner saying 'what a terrible child', so I turned and poked my tongue out at them. Unfortunately, my mother saw me and gave me a real slap, so I started bawling again until one of the hairdressers had the great idea of shoving a lollipop into my gob. I was quite happy with the lollipop and let the poor woman go ahead with the scissors, but when I saw what I looked like with one half lopped off I started to roar! They then bought me Coca Cola, chocolate and the offer of any sweet I could think of if I would just stop roaring and let the hairdresser finish the job. They finally got me with an offer of hard cash, my mother holding up a ten-bob note! 'You'll give that ten-bob note straight back to me, ye little bitch,' Mum said as we walked home. I handed it over straight away, because she was mad at me for making such a great show of her in the hairdresser's. She could never stay angry for long, though, and she was soon putting on funny voices and pretending she didn't know who I was because I looked so different with my lopsided haircut. I was screeching with laughter and shouting, 'It's me! It's me, the bab!' We played the game for the next few weeks.

I think she was really laughing at the haircut, which in the whole history of haircuts was right up there with an *Edward Scissorhands* creation. I can't blame her for getting my hair cut short, because hair-washing days took three adults: two to hold me face-up on the draining board and one to do the actual shampooing and rinsing. This could often prove problematic, because only a trusted few could do the actual shampooing and my mother wasn't one of them! I think they gave up on the brushing altogether unless one of my aunts was visiting and got control of the hairbrush.

And, sadly, the haircut had become necessary. My big brother had got hold of a pair of scissors and cut off a big chunk of hair in the middle of my scalp. Contrary to what all my mother's caring friends said (she had friends in those days), the tuft continued growing upwards in a straight line. Colin and I thought it was hilarious, but I would pretend to cry about my beautiful hair if Mum was looking and if he was still laughing he would get a belt round the ear. He used to do the same to me for other things, and she would take his side more than mine because he was her favourite, but it didn't matter because I was Dad's.

For the big things, Colin and I never told on each other. We shared a room when we were really small, and we would lie in bed conspiring about who would do what for who if we kept our traps shut. The ultimate punishment was being a slave. When Colin put up a dartboard and invited his pals round and a dart accidentally went through my thumb, he had to be my slave for two weeks. If he didn't do what I said, I would point at my thumb and pretend to cry. That usually did it! He never had much luck when it was my turn to be his servant, because I didn't have the good character or the good grace to keep my part of the bargain, so it would end up in a big fight again with both of us getting yelled at.

I don't think Colin liked having me around with him all the time, because he always had to look after me. We lived at 555 Stroud Road, Virginia Water, exactly opposite Holloway Sanatorium. Dad was a chef there with a white uniform and a tall white hat, and Mum was a nurse with a stash of crisp white unfolded nurse's hats that she kept hidden in the bottom drawer of her dressing table. I wasn't supposed to know where they were, because I kept getting my mucky mitts on them and she would chase me round the house threatening to kill me if I ever touched them again.

The house we lived in belonged to a man named Bill Lucas, and he lived there with us. He was very tall with dark hair and a big bald patch in the middle, and he always used to make us laugh. When he had his breakfast in the morning, Colin and I would hide under the table, steal his toast soldiers and dip them in his egg when he wasn't looking, then he would chase us all around the house with a wooden spoon while we squealed and giggled. He used to call me 'Baggy Pants', because I was always too busy to get to the loo in time and my soggy pants used to hang around my knees. If I was out playing, I used to just take them off and throw them away. Nearly every night Mum or Dad had to lead me down the garden with a torch to see where I had chucked them, because I could never remember. The garden was huge and long with loads of vegetables and sweet peas growing on either side of the path. Colin and I used to love helping Bill with his gardening, and we would spend hours with him, mostly getting in the way, I think. He even gave Colin a little patch of ground to grow things, and when he saw my bottom lip trembling he said I could grow stuff too. We planted the flower seeds very carefully, and we would get up as soon as it was light to water them and see if they had grown.

I was never treated any differently to Colin because I was a girl. There were only 11 months between us, and I had shadowed him from the moment I could toddle. My tantrums, and maybe my parents' forward thinking, ensured that I was allowed to do anything he was allowed to do. Although they hadn't gone so far as to have us baptised as Winona or River, they had sort of caught on to the whole '60s revolution and did their own thing. Colin and I were totally equal, apart from him being slightly older. Dad did try to do separate 'boy' things with Colin, like go fishing in the lakes or wake him up at three o'clock in the morning to come down and watch the Cassius Clay fight, whispering to each other so they didn't wake me up, but if I got a whiff of what they were up to I would tag along.

Our house sat in the middle of a red-brick terrace that faced Holloway Sanatorium. There were bigger houses at the end of the rows, further back from the path. Our house was big and small at the same time. It was small on the outside, but it went right the way back and out onto a long, narrow garden, then some bushes, then the paddock. As you came in the front door, the front room was the first door on the left. It wasn't a very big room, but it had a bay window that pushed out towards the small front garden. In the bay was a large wooden table covered with a green velour tablecloth with tassels at each corner. There was a big brown leather sofa against the back wall and a large leather armchair that belonged to Bill. On the wall facing the door was a walnut, glass-doored cabinet that contained a china tea service that I wasn't allowed to touch because I was a clumsy little mare.

The front hall led down into the main living area, which was a large room with a table and chairs in the middle, armchairs in the corners, a clothes horse and a couple of odd armchairs by the fireplace and a sink unit with a draining board along the back wall. The kitchen area spilled over into a small corridor that led out to the lavatory, the yard and then into the garden. When I had measles, Dad and Bill pushed the two armchairs together and made a bed for me with a sheet over the top to stop the light from hurting my eyes.

My mother used to dress me beautifully in those days; I think I was the little doll she never had. Not that she had much success: I hated having my hair brushed and mud and stones were my favourite toys. She would sign up for credit everywhere and scour the second-hand shops and the jumble sales. I had loads of dresses, but they didn't matter to me one jot. I had more important things to do, like make mud pies.

The world was so much fun then. We didn't have babysitters; no one did. Our house backed onto the paddock, a large area of greenery surrounded by nurses' homes with lanes leading off to Virginia Water train station, Egham, Thorpe and Lyne Place, and it was all the personal playground of our little gang – or, more accurately, Colin's little gang, made up of kids whose parents worked at Holloway. From the children of doctors to the children of domestics, and whatever nationality you were, if you could make mud pies, you were in. I was the unwelcome little sister who Colin felt obliged to look after. But he had strict rules on how I could behave: I was not allowed to climb trees or throw mud pies, because I was a girl. I was allowed to make the mud pies as ammo, but I was not allowed to actually throw them at anyone. I put up with this for a while, but one day when Colin got my mad up I threw one at him. We had a rift in the gang for a couple of days, because I took Ray Price* and Hans Schmitt* with me. Ray was an older boy who lived a few doors away, and who hadn't started school yet because, according to my mum, he was 'a bit thick in the head'. Hans was about my age, and he wore lederhosen and spoke with a funny accent. I liked them two best, because they were easy to boss around.

Ray lived a few doors down on the left in a big, posh 1930s house with a front parlour. I loved going round to his house, because his mum was always in and she wore an apron all day long. She would always invite me in and ask if I wanted to go into the parlour room and have a cup of tea. Ray and I used to have to sit on the big armchairs nicely and not swing our legs, because it damaged the chairs, while his mum made us tea and sandwiches. She never shouted or threatened to beat the daylights out of us, so I always kept my voice down and stayed on my best behaviour because she was so kind. I loved it when she would bring in a full tray loaded with a proper china teapot and tea set and a three-tier cake stand with delicate paste and cucumber sandwiches with the crusts cut off, then cake and scones, all home-made. She was the perfect hostess and would say to me and Ray, 'Shall I pour?' But I could see her wince when I fumbled to put my sugar spoon into the delicate little bowl, chinking almost every cup and saucer on the way. Then I would have to balance the loaded spoon back over the rest of her best china with my shaking, dirty, clumsy mitts. She eventually persuaded me, ever so politely, that two sugars could be just as nice as six, but I think she only said that because I was spilling so much of it over her best rug.

I always enjoyed Mrs Price's company, nearly as much I enjoyed Ray's. She had a huge, highly polished display cabinet in her parlour that was filled with all sorts of china and trinkets. I would listen in awe as she delicately removed one precious object at a time to show me and lovingly described its history. She told such great stories that I would beg her to tell me them again and again, and I would follow her as she went around in her Marigolds polishing things, then peeling potatoes and vegetables, preparing for when Mr Price was due home. I would hang on in there until she laughingly shooed me out the door and told me to come back another day.

Of course, I loved the food, too; all we had to eat at home was bread, jam and maybe sugar if no one was looking. And we always had butter, never margarine. I remember Mum screaming at a neighbour that, 'Yer kids are dragged up, not brought up,' and to add extra venom, she yelled, 'And we wouldn't lower ourselves to eat margarine, ye stingy aul bitch – yeah, you were seen!' She could never keep up her posh voice when she was having a row with anyone, which was often because she could never keep her evil thoughts to herself.

She started a rumour that the local hairdressing salon was using dog shampoo instead of proper shampoo and was charging a fortune for it. For weeks, we had all sorts of irate hairdressers, as well as their husbands and an assortment of relatives, shouting outside our front door that Mum was off her head and should be locked up. Mum didn't care, she loved having a row – I think she thoroughly enjoyed them. Sometimes we kids got involved and turned against each other, shouting things like 'your mum's got a moustache' or 'your mum's got an arse bigger than our sofa'. Sometimes they would say 'your mum's the talk of the neighbourhood'. I didn't care because she was much, much prettier than their mums, and she was much younger, too. She wore nicer clothes than them as well, and she would always put the radio on full blast so the three of us could dance and sing and have a laugh. Their mums were old and grey, and they wore aprons and peeled potatoes all day long, and they were boring.

We kids could never stay enemies for long, though, because there was too much fun to be had, and I could always make Ray or Hans laugh, even if they were trying their hardest to keep a straight face and not talk to me.

Hans was my other best friend; I had nabbed him for myself when the other kids were being horrible to him. I liked him because he was different, and I loved dragging him along to meet people and telling them his name. I would stand still and give it a minute to sink in, and then I would say bold as brass that he was a German. I couldn't wait to see the look of shock and horror on their faces as I said it. It was the early 1960s, and the quaint folk who lived in the sleepy suburb of Virginia Water hadn't quite reached the 'forgive and forget' stage when it came to thinking about the war. Other nationalities, or even other colours, didn't seem to bother them a jot, but some were still deeply suspicious of Germans, even of little ones in lederhosen. My parents weren't bothered a bit that Hans was German; he was just another kid running in and out of the house with the rest of us. Mum was like me and loved his strange accent, but she didn't believe me at all when I told her about his strange habit of sucking his thumb and holding on to you by the earlobe when you sat to watch the telly, until he did it to her. I was used to it, of course; I had been around to his house loads of times and I had seen him do it to his mother and his father, and they didn't bat an eyelid, so when we snuggled up together on the chair and he grabbed hold of my lug, I kept my trap shut and I felt like I was part of the family.

I drummed it into Mum, of course, that she was to act as though it was the most normal thing in the world and not say anything. She promised faithfully that she would and stifled her giggles when Hans grabbed her ear. Against my better nature, and following lots of promises from her, she drew me and Colin in and we decided to set Dad up. Dad suspected nothing as I happily gave up my seat next to him on the sofa, allowing Hans to sit there instead, and, as we three looked on gleefully, true to form Hans relaxed, put his thumb in his mouth and grabbed Dad's earlobe. The look on Dad's face was priceless and the three of us collapsed in laughter.

I was a bit disappointed not to get a shocked reaction from Mum and Dad about my German friend, because they knew a lot about Germany and the war. They were always arguing about it, especially when they were drinking. Dad always used to win, though, because he knew loads about the war. The war started when he was a kid and he was too young to join up, but his older brother was in the army and Dad kept a great big map of the world in his room and he would mark off all the battles. His family used to listen to the news all huddled around the radio, and they all had to keep quiet as Winston Churchill spoke. Dad used to get tears in his eyes when he quoted Churchill's iconic words 'we will fight them on the beaches' and 'we will never surrender', and he would do the voice and all the actions too, and Colin and I would beg him to do it again. Then he would sigh and shake his head at the memory.

Hans was happy to go along with any mischief I planned and even came up with several new ruses of his own. He didn't speak to other people very much. I don't know if that was because of the language barrier or the fact that I would never let him get a word in. I think he must have had good English, though, because we would chat and giggle between ourselves for hours on end. I even managed to persuade his very reluctant parents to let me come and stay at his house for the night. I loved visiting his house; it was one of the most exciting houses I had ever seen. Everything was square and it was all so posh and clean, with loads of space. Everyone I knew lived in poky old houses like ours. I was dying to get inside those doors and mooch around. Everything was new and shiny and modern. They even had those curtains with a cord that you pulled and then the curtains would close by themselves, like the ones in the James Bond films that you saw at the pictures. Boy, was I dying to get my mitts on those!

I was, of course, on my very best behaviour when my mother dropped me off with my little suitcase. She behaved herself too, and profusely thanked Hans's parents in her best posh accent for inviting me. I thought it was odd that she didn't stay talking for long and I wondered if she would come to collect me the next day. But I wasn't bothered at all; I had this amazing house to explore. Unfortunately, all thoughts of that were quickly wiped away when Hans's father appeared as we started to walk towards the bedroom. 'Wait in the hallway,' he shouted in his clipped German accent. Hans and I immediately did as he said and stood still. I tried to stifle a giggle, but Hans threw me a look that said, 'Don't you dare!' His father told us to stand still and be quiet as he read out a list of rules, which included not going into rooms that were strictly forbidden. He then walked us around the house and pointed out the forbidden doors. To me, it just made them all the more enticing, but I had promised Mum that I would behave, so I decided to put my exploring plans on hold and stay on my best behaviour. Besides, Hans's father frightened the bejesus out of me.

We did have an evening of organised games and I remember enjoying them immensely, and Hans's parents didn't turn out to be half as scary as I had imagined them to be. They tucked us into two single beds in Hans's room. 'No talking, no giggling,' shouted his father in a voice that sounded like he really meant it. By the time he shut the door I was ready to giggle so much I thought I would burst. Hans was in the same mood, and before long we were setting each other up with challenges to see who lasted longest while the other one tried to make them laugh, and the more his parents shouted, the more we struggled to hold back the urge to giggle. Eventually, his exasperated father came to the room and said if we carried on we would have to stand in the corner. This only made us laugh all the more until, left with no other option, he ordered the pair of us into opposite corners of the hallway and made us face the walls. As punishments go, it wasn't up to much; neither party was willing to admit defeat! I think in honesty the parents won, or simply forgot we were out there, because we woke up on our pillows in the hallway. But it might be that we weakened them by getting them to provide pillows.

In our life in Virginia Water, everyone was equal: boys, girls, those of different colours and nationalities and those with different accents. The majority of the hospital staff were 'foreign' – though I wasn't to learn that word until many years later. There were all sorts of nationalities: Indian, Polish, African, Chinese, Scottish, Irish, even German – it was like a small international community based around the mighty gothic sanatorium, living in harmony. Doctors' children played with kitchen workers' children.

However, my mother was not as egalitarian as my father. Although she didn't mind me playing with Hans, she definitely used to think we were superior to the black and Indian families – but only when Dad was out of earshot. I don't think she was really racist, though, because she thought we were superior to everybody. We weren't really; in fact, I think we were pretty near the bottom of the ladder socially. The Irish and Scottish seemed to have their own community within a community: the heavy-drinking, deep philosophy-talking and partying Celts, who, of course, always loved a sing-song. I think that is why there have never been any direct wars between Ireland and Scotland – well, none that I know of – because even though they will spend the whole night arguing to the death and may even come to blows, they always end up singing 'Danny Boy' and are best friends again by the time they get to the 'I love you so' bit.

Well, maybe Mum was a bit a racist, but she never used to say anything to anyone's faces. She would never use someone's race or a disability against them even in a row, but apart from that pretty much anything went. And she always had an uncanny knack of latching on to someone's weak spot in an instant, storing it and annotating it in her head for future use. Colin and I used to will strangers not to show any weakness because we knew what she was like.

The only girl I ever played with was Ivy Kabir. She was one of three daughters of one of the Indian doctors who worked in Holloway. We got to know the entire family and referred to them as 'the Ivy Kabirs'. I don't know why the name stuck; I think it was because Ivy was the first one I introduced to my mum and the name tickled her. They lived in a big corner house on Stroud Road with large wooden gates leading into its driveway. And they even had a car. Ivy used to say to me, 'Fer feck's sake [I taught her to swear], don't knock on the door when Dad's car is there.' This may have been a keep-me-out tactic, because his car was always there; he only worked across the road. I would always try to find any excuse to go and knock for them, because when their dad wasn't home they welcomed me in, their mum as well. I was always drawn to the wonderful exotic smell of their cooking, and their mum cooked great big feasts every day. Their mum would tolerate me in the kitchen and let me try the things she was cooking, but I could never quite wangle my way into their family dinners.

When their dad was out, the place was a dream. They would show me their beautiful bedrooms, and the most sacred place of all (strictly forbidden in every child's home), their parents' bedroom. Mrs K owned a beautiful wardrobe of saris in bright, vibrant colours, many covered in diamonds and gold. I was in awe of their sheer beauty. To me, Mrs K looked like a beautiful exotic princess. She had the longest hair I had ever seen, and it was ebony black and always brushed to a glowing sheen. Her saris were dazzling, and she even showed me how to put one on once. She wore bangles and big earrings and they shimmered against her beautiful brown skin. I remember trying to have a dig at Mum once by telling her how fabulous Mrs K was. 'She cooks things all day long, you know,' I told Mum, but she was hardly paying attention. 'And she has dozens of saris covered in diamonds and pearls,' I told her, and looked sadly at my mum's tight black slacks and crisp white blouse. She got her own back on me by telling me to tell Mrs K that bacon rashers were on offer in Hobson's, but Mrs K just laughed when I told her.

I found the Kabir house fascinating. Mrs Kabir was so dignified and elegant, and I never once heard her swear or saw her whack a child around the head. Mrs K never got involved in the neighbourhood gossip; she would always smile and change the subject. I respected her; I never once saw her shout or get ruffled by anything. She was so completely different from the other residents who came from the row of workers' cottages that faced Holloway Sanatorium. As well as the usual tantalising food smells, the Kabirs' house was tastefully decorated and contained captivating art and objects that I had never seen before. And I was so surprised to find that they ate with their hands and not knives and forks. Of course, I couldn't keep that juicy bit of gossip to myself for love nor money and I blabbered it out to everyone, even to the old lady who ran the sweet shop. I don't think Mrs K was very happy to see me when I went back. I liked Konnie Kabir the best. I think she was about the same age as me. Some mornings, I used to snuggle into bed with my mum when she came in from night duty, and sometimes Konnie would come running in through the back door and jump in as well. 'Don't let her in!' I used to shout to Mum. 'Her bum's freezing!' That always used to make Mum laugh; then she would throw the pair of us out.

Mr and Mrs K never used to go to the clubhouse, which was in the middle of Stroud Road, set back from the terraces. It was a proper old drinking establishment that stank of beer and fags, and where children were 'Strictly Prohibited'. If a child did get in, there was a long walk from the door across the beer-sodden carpet, then past the comfy chairs and tables, to get to the bar, with all the grown-ups looking daggers at you. Above the bar hung a spooky painting of an old man with eyes that followed you everywhere, like he knew exactly what you were doing and thinking. I think it was to scare the bejesus out of us and keep us away, but it had the opposite effect on me. Because I found it so fascinating, I would drag every kid I could find to come and take a look at the fella with the eyes.

The clubhouse was really for the hospital staff, and grown men and women would come out late in the afternoon, crying and singing 'take me home to Eire' songs. We kids always knew they were good to cadge a few sixpences from, especially if you could sing 'Lovely Leitrim' all the way through while looking angelic.

We were always dreaming up money-making schemes. We would make a hole in a leaf and push a daisy through so it looked pretty, then sell each one for a penny. For a while, we used to get the nurses coming off duty to buy them, but they lost interest and after that they just used to chase us with their cloaks held out like vampires, trying to catch us and sweep us up in their capes. We loved that game and tormented them until one of the nursing sisters came out and told us to clear off or she would tell our parents. Strangely, this usually worked.

I don't remember whose idea it was to hijack the hospital's bakery delivery man, but it worked a treat. We got the idea from the films we saw at the staff cinema, which everyone used to go to. I remember the four of us going along there to see cowboy films and James Bond films and happily chatting about them all the way home. Dad and Colin used to love all the blood and guts and moaned and groaned when the hero and heroine got all soppy and interrupted the violence. Mum and I loved the stories and would try to sing the songs, and Colin and Dad would cover their ears and say we sounded like strangled cats, especially when we sang 'From Russia with Love'. I hated the violent bits in the films and always sat next to Dad so I could look away and hide under his arm until he told me it was safe to come out. Colin used to memorise those parts, though, so he could torment me later, especially the scene with the maggots in *Ben-Hur*.

We kids got to see a lot of cowboy and Indian films, so we thought we would spring an Apache Indian raid on the bakery man. Even the parents assisted with our costumes. 'Yes, you can have me fecking scarf,' my mother said. 'Now feck off.' We held a proper powwow and decided on our tactics. I think Colin was in charge, because I wasn't allowed to climb trees. But after a quick threat to tell Dad what we were up to, he agreed that I could climb up as far as the first branch, but no more. The ambush was thoroughly worth the planning: we were rewarded with cakes and buns and anything else we demanded. We held the delivery man, Tom Banner, hostage until he bribed us into going away. Tom soon became our friend and I think he enjoyed the game for a while, but eventually the only thing he gave us was a loaf of plain bread. We attacked even that as if it was the first crumb we had had for days, though it wasn't, it was just the prize.

I think we all got bored with it in the end, but as summer moved into autumn we hit the jackpot with 'Penny for the Guy'. 'Can we borrow Linda's old pram, Mum?' Colin shouted up the stairs.

'Take what the feck you like,' she shouted back. 'And take her with you!' Mum was always trying to get sleep during the day because she worked nights. Dad worked days, so they rarely used to see each other, or very much of us children.

The pram had long been abandoned in the back yard and was rusting along with the other old junk. Colin and his pals set about getting the pram working and polishing the wheels until they were gleaming. 'I am not getting into that thing until you prove to me there are no spiders,' I growled at Colin.

'You saw us clean it enough times to know there aren't any,' he snarled back. 'And if you don't get in, you're not coming.' He had used the ultimate threat. I was so obsessed with the spiders that I didn't bother to think about him letting go of the pram as we went down the steep hill towards the train station.

The first few times 'Penny for the Guy' worked out fine and I could up the profits with my 'they're just about to burn me at the stake' look. However, eventually, Mum got wind of what was going on, probably from that Mrs Jarvis at number 47, who always stuck her big hooter into everything, and Mum was running down from the top of the hill shouting that she was going to fecking kill us. In fright, Colin let go of the pram, sending me hurtling towards certain death, but he couldn't make up his mind which way to run. Happily, he decided to go with chasing the pram, but before my runaway pram had got very much further some kindly home-going commuter who was walking up the hill stopped the pram in its tracks. We all ended up in a heap, with Mum picking Colin up by the scruff of the neck and threatening to break every bone in his body. She didn't mean it, of course, but she would often play the stern mother in front of other people, letting them think that she was a strict and caring parent. She dragged the pair of us home, holding on to our hands and shouting all the ways in which she was going to kill us, loud enough for all the neighbours to hear, and she threw in a clip round the head for Colin when we went past number 47, so the old biddy who lived there would see what a strict mother she was.

There was always so much to do in and around Virginia Water, and nowhere was out of bounds. In the summer there was an open-air swimming pool, and I vividly remember spending entire summers there. It was always packed on hot, sunny days and we kids loved it. We were told to stay near the shallow end at all times, and we did, on the whole. Dad would get in with us and try to teach us to swim. It was Colin's turn on the day of our near demise! As Dad held Colin in the shallow end, I ran to see a friend at the other end of the pool, doing the opposite of everything I had been told. Naturally, I slipped and fell in and must have let out a hell of a shriek, because almost everyone in and around the pool reacted. The fellow on the diving board dived straight in and headed at top speed towards me, and Dad chucked Colin on the pool steps and swam my way too. Unfortunately, Colin slipped off of the steps and back into the water, so the pair of us ended up having water pumped out of us at the side of the pool.

We kids always used to meet in the paddock and decide on our next escapade there. From Sandy Lane to Stroud Road, the area was our playground. We always had trees to climb, conkers to collect or other kids' parents to pester. One time we even found a huge barrel of soot. We thought it would be just as good as the sand on a beach and used a small bucket to make soot castles, but they didn't hold, so we just spent the rest of the day chucking it at each other. Dad was horrified when we turned up at the back door – all he could see were the whites of our eyes. He got the hose out.

The only time we ever got into any real trouble was when Colin decided to use a five-pound note he found on the kitchen table to pay Ray to look after me when he started school. We had a gang meeting, where I had to keep my trap shut, while they decided on the safest place to keep the five-pound note. The only thing they could agree on was that neither of them could be trusted with it. I could have told them that. It was eventually decided that they would use one of Dad's old baccy tins to put the five-pound note in and then bury it in the paddock. Dad had come in from an early shift and chucked his wages and baccy tin on the kitchen table before going upstairs for a snooze. We made sure his baccy was safely wrapped in foil before taking the tin and the five-pound note, and off we went. We knew Dad would think it was a good idea getting Ray to look after me, so we were sure he wouldn't mind. But the burying of the tin turned into a fiasco, and fights broke out about who should do the burying and who should be allowed to see where it was buried. We eventually agreed that there was no practical way of hiding where we'd put it from the less trustworthy kids, because they could still look through the bushes and peep. By this time, we had moved the tin many times and wanted to get home because it was getting dark. It never occurred to us that what we had done was wrong, but, just in case, we swore a pact never to tell anyone.

When we got home there was a crowd outside our house, including a policeman. Someone had walked in through the back door and stolen Frank Hutton's wages off the kitchen table! The neighbours were outraged. No one ever locked their doors; theft was unheard of in our tightly knit hospital community. 'Don't you blab,' I whispered to Colin when we realised what was going on.

'It was you, you little bitch!' my mother yelled at me, but the policeman had grabbed my hand before she could reach me. He bent down and asked me firmly and sternly, did I know what had happened to the money? His black policeman's uniform scared me. I felt my bottom lip quivering, and before I knew it I was crying and confessing everything. I half wanted to tell on Colin and say it was his idea, but I didn't, even though he was a pig. The adults were more concerned with finding out where exactly in the field we'd buried the money before it became too dark to search for it. Some even went home and got torches. The trouble was that Colin, Ray and I were all giving different stories and different places, because we had spent the whole afternoon burying it and digging it up again, so that in the end we didn't have a clue where it was. The five-pound note never was found.

Colin was due to start school shortly after that, and I was bereft. It was all so unfair – I screamed, shouted and cried myself to sleep for weeks over the fact that Colin was starting school and I wasn't. Colin was only 11 months older than me, not even a full year. I was inconsolable. Friends and neighbours went out of their way to be nice to me. Even the woman in the sweet shop gave me a free sweet because she had never seen such a sad face.

Eventually, execution day arrived. Colin was going out of his way to torment me with his new school uniform, and Mum eventually said, 'For feck's sake, don't hit him or you'll get blood on his shirt.' This just made Colin act up even more, because he knew I wouldn't dare defy Mum when she was in one of those moods. Mum had each of us by the hand as she walked towards the school, with me and Colin trying to drag back so we could poke our tongues out at each other. The sight of all the new kids in their uniforms with their satchels and lining up in their classes in the playground was more than I could bear. My bottom lip had been trembling for ages, and the sight of the beautiful Miss Robinson in her smart suit, delicate string of pearls and perfect Audrey Hepburn updo was simply too much. I had heard that Miss Robinson, who ran the infants' class, kept a beautiful box in her desk. It was pink and tied up with ribbons. Now I would never see it! I couldn't hold back any longer and I roared like a banshee, and every silent line of children queuing up in front of the classrooms turned and stared. The headmaster, Mr Paterson, started walking across the playground. He looked furious, as if to say, 'Are you ever going to shut that brat up?' Miss Robinson saved the day by grabbing me by the hand and leading me up to the steps of her classroom prefab. She made her class wait outside as she led me around the classroom, showing me all the letters and drawings on the wall. 'Can I be teacher's pet?' I asked. I'd heard all about teachers' pets, and I desperately wanted to be one.

'You can,' she said, squeezing my hand. 'The year will go by in no time.' When she said the word 'year', my bottom lip started to tremble again – a year was for ever when you were only three and a half. I tried to hold the tears back, but I couldn't stop them. She bent down and used her own handkerchief to dry my eyes, and said, 'Come on, I have got something very special to show you.' Then she led me by the hand towards her desk and unlocked the bottom drawer. And there it was. It was the most beautiful box I had ever seen! Covered in red satin, it was studded with sparkling jewels that twinkled in the sunlight, and it was tied up with a big red bow. I had heard all about it but thought the kids were making it up. But everything they had said was true! She lifted the lid and offered me a sweet from the secret treasure box. I was in heaven as I carefully unwrapped the sweet and put it in my mouth. That calmed me down for a little while – well, at least until all the kids went into their classrooms and Mum and I were alone in the playground. That was enough to start me roaring again, and I remember Mum tucking me kicking and screaming under her arm as she carried me across the empty playground and all the way home.

But she wasn't angry with me; in fact, she was doing her best to make me laugh. I helped her to tidy up when we got home, and then she took me into the front room to lie on the leather sofa with her as she put the radio on for *Listen with Mother*. I loved lying next to her, listening to the stories, and when the nice lady said, 'Are you sitting comfortably?' me and Mum would shout, 'Yes, we are,' as we lay on the sofa giggling. I always wanted to listen to every word of the story, but she would mess about and make me giggle so much that I kept missing bits of it. I also really liked it when she had the country-and-western songs blaring out, and I especially loved it when Hank Locklin came on the radio, because we had made up a game to play where we would lie down and sing along with him, and then when he got to the line 'Please help me, I'm falling', we would roll off the sofa and onto the floor, play-fight and then scramble back onto the sofa for when he sang it again.

Dad was late coming home from work that day, and Colin and I were sitting outside on the wall waiting for him. Colin wanted to boast about his first day at school. I just wanted a cuddle. As we saw him approaching from the wrong direction, we could see that he had a huge parcel under his arm all wrapped up in brown paper and string. We begged and pleaded with him to tell us what it was, but he kept saying, 'Hold on now, hold on,' and teasing us by making us wait. I could hardly contain my excitement when he tore the paper off to reveal a blackboard! And he had chalk, too, so every day Colin could come home from school and tell us everything he learned, and he would do it all again on the blackboard for me. Mum, Dad and even Colin were smiling, but I was suspicious and could feel my bottom lip trembling. 'But what about the little bottles of milk?' I blubbed. Then Colin said Mum would bring some in after playtime. Yes, we were going to have proper playtimes as well, and Dad would whistle to call us back in, because he didn't have a real whistle. It was the happiest day of my life. And even though I didn't like Mum or Colin, they could be nice sometimes.

Chapter 20
Lyne Place

The second home I remember was Lyne Place. It was still in Virginia Water, but it was out in the sticks, miles from anywhere. Colin and I were both going to school by then, St Ann's primary school at the top of Stroud Road.

We had eventually left Bill and 555 Stroud Road to move into a house of our very own. It was such an exciting time, and Colin and I were going to get a bedroom each! It was a huge red-brick house in the middle of nowhere. I don't think it was *the* Lyne Place (the area was named after a Lyne Place Manor), but we always called it that. Colin and I loved it; we could run up and down the stairs and from room to room, shouting as much as we liked, with no fear of waking Uncle Bill.

It was an old semi-detached house with a killer staircase that just seemed to drop off from the top step. 'If yeez fall and break your necks, don't come running to me,' Mum used to shout at us when we were running up and down them. The stairs faced the front door, and on the left was the living room. A door led off from there into the kitchen, and then the bathroom came off from that. The kitchen was large with a red-brick floor, butler sink and an oblong wooden table.

I was a 'little bugger' with my food and hardly liked anything other than spuds. Even then, if Dad was making mash he would find me, drag me into the kitchen and make me watch him push the potatoes through a sieve, so that I had proof positive that there were absolutely no lumps. Mum just used to say, 'If she won't eat them, she can bleddy go without.' I definitely didn't like anything green, so most vegetables were out, and after having watched Ben-Hur eating bread with maggots I was so traumatised that I went off bread too.

Dad was terrified that I was dying of starvation because I was so small and skinny, and Mum used to make me and Colin eggnogs to top up our diets. The eggnogs weren't alcoholic; they were made of raw eggs beaten with milk and sugar. They actually tasted really nice, and I would have one of them when all else failed. Colin didn't need them really, because he used to eat everything, even if he didn't like it, just to make me look worse. He even ate liver, and I cracked up laughing, watching him go green around the gills and trying to say, 'Mmmmm.'

One row over food led to me getting a thump around the ear and Mum telling me to go without. It wasn't one of her 'playing' thumps, either. I hated her but wasn't going to give in, so I sulked for a while and then, when she wasn't looking, I went out to the kitchen to see what I could find. We didn't have a fridge and our food was kept in a wooden cabinet that leaned up against the wall. It had two big cupboards at the bottom, a row of shelves and then a glass bit at the top with sliding doors. I was wondering what was in a bowl on one of the shelves I couldn't reach, so I stood as high as I could on my tiptoes and reached up. Unfortunately, the bowl contained the remains of a tin of peas and the lot came crashing down over my head. I let out such a scream that Mum and Colin came running, and as I stood there with green juice running down into my eyes the pair of them fell on the floor laughing.

I was outraged and decided there and then to run away for ever. 'Ye'll never see me again!' I shouted as I ran out of the door, fighting back the tears because I wouldn't give them the pleasure of seeing me cry. I ran across the road and off into the woods, deciding I was going to live there for ever more, just like Snow White. Of course,

I didn't really believe I would find a tiny house with seven tiny little men any more than I believed in fairies, but I always hoped and used to explore the woods for hours.

If you went really deep into the woods, you would sometimes find a whole field of bluebells. I had no idea what 'seasonal' meant; I only knew that when I first found it I was awestruck! It was the most beautiful sight I had ever seen and I doubted anyone else in the world had ever seen anything like it before. I had run home screaming with excitement and dragged Mum and Colin and Dad to come and look at it. 'It's only flowers,' said Colin, but Mum told him to shut his gob.

As I sat in the middle of the bluebells, picking peas out of my hair, I thought about Mum and how on the days when I liked her I would go and pick her a bunch of bluebells. But on that day I was determined to teach her and Colin a lesson by never coming home. 'They'll soon miss me,' I thought. After about 20 minutes, when no one came, I thought I might go home for a little while, but I definitely wouldn't stay. But if I did decide to stay, I wasn't going to speak to those two. As it was, I had to hover in the doorway for ages before they spoke to me, but it was definitely Colin who spoke first, as I reminded him when we had a fight later.

We didn't have any neighbours other than the strange women who lived in the house attached to ours. Apart from them, there wasn't another house for miles. We used to call them 'the Headscarves' because there only seemed to be women living there and they used to pull their headscarves down and walk away quickly when they saw us. I think it was because Mum told them to 'feck off' on the day we moved in. Mum used to have to wait for them to go out before she could put the record player on loud, because they would moan and tell Dad. Colin and I used to take it in turns to keep a lookout for them and would delight in running in to Mum shouting, 'The Headscarves are coming! The Headscarves are coming!', so she could turn the music down.

We had an old record player at the time and Mum would delight in buying records even though Dad would moan and say we couldn't afford them. Dad thought the Beatles were scruffy sods with their long hair and that the Rolling Stones were even worse, especially that Mick Jagger. Dad always wore his hair short with a long bit on the top that he would smother in Brylcreem and then comb back into a quiff.

Most of Mum's records were country and western, though, and she would play them all the time, singing along with Patsy Cline and Hank Locklin. Colin and I used to join in, too, singing along at the top of our voices, especially when the Headscarves were out. All those records would come out whenever Mum and Dad had a drink, and they both used to love to sing along and dance and sing to each other when the soppy ones came on. Dad used to pretend that he didn't like country and western, but he did really, because he used to sing along to Jim Reeves. He was always a bit behind, though, because he used to do the arm movements, sway his head and look all goo-goo eyes at Mum when he sang 'I Love You Because'.

We also had a black and white television, and our favourite programmes were *Juke Box Jury* and *Top of the Pops*. 'Oi'll give it five,' Mum used to say in a funny voice, imitating one of the presenters, and Mum and Colin and I would sing along while Dad would sit there tutting. We all had to keep quiet when the news came on, but none of us could ever keep our traps shut so Dad used to kick us out of the room. I once pretended I liked the news so I could stay and sit with him, but I couldn't keep it up for very long because I didn't know what they were talking about.

When Cassius Clay was fighting Sonny Liston, Dad arranged to set the alarm to go off in the middle of the night so that he and Colin could get up to watch the fight. I wanted to get up and watch it as well and said it wasn't fair that I couldn't just because I was a girl. Dad said it wasn't because I was a girl; it was because I never stopped chattering and fidgeting and I would spoil it for everyone. 'You come and get in with me and never mind them,' Mum said when I told her all about it.

But I couldn't ignore it; everyone was talking about the 'big fight' everywhere we went. Mum loved Cassius Clay, much more than

Dad did. She said it was because he was so good-looking, and she loved telling people that, especially the old biddies in the shop, who thought she was scandalous. It used to make her giggle when she gave them something to talk about.

Apart from the Headscarves, there were no other people around, and there wasn't a shop, a pub or a soul for miles. The only time we saw people was when the potato pickers turned up in the fields behind us, and then Mum would get herself a job and join in with them. Colin and I used to go and help her sometimes, because the more pallets you filled the more money you got. We used to love helping and the bosses didn't mind, but we would usually end up fighting, chasing moles or talking too much and getting on the other workers' nerves and Mum would have to send us home.

To get to the nearest shops in Virginia Water, you had to walk all the way down Lyne Road, cross the stile into the first fields, follow the narrow walkway across a wooden bridge over a stream, go through the thick woods into the next field, then walk down Sandy Lane and along Trumpington Road. We all had to do it, Dad going off to his shifts at Holloway and me and Colin to get to school.

At the time of the Great Train Robbery, Dad thought he had encountered the robbers in the woods on his way home from work. It had been pitch black and he had seen a group of men sitting around a fire. He didn't go too close to them, just hurried by, and he wasn't going to report it to the police because he wanted them to get away with it. Everyone did. Wherever you went, people were talking about it and dreaming up all the things they would do if they had all that money. They said the robbers were using the notes to light their fags and even played Monopoly using real money.

I used to love walking through the fields and along the country paths; actually, I think we all did. We even used to go on big, long walks, even if we didn't have to. We once found a tree with cobnuts that we could just help ourselves to, and on many of our walks we were just trying to find it again, because no one could ever remember where it was. 'It's this way,' Dad would shout if we reached a crossroads.

'No, it's not, it's this way,' Mum would reply, then we would all end up pretending to be the Scarecrow from *The Wizard of Oz*, crossing our arms over and laughing. If Mum and Dad really got lost, they would ask me and Colin, though mainly Colin because I was usually 'away with the fairies' and they would never believe a word I said.

It was usually dark as we made our way home and Mum put the fear of God into me by telling all of us that bats can bump into you and get tangled in your hair. One night when we returned from a walk, one flew in through the kitchen window, or it might just have flown past the window, but Mum and I starting screaming for dear life until Dad came to the rescue.

Eventually, Dad bought a scooter. They were all the rage at the time, but for Dad it was an absolute necessity. I have no idea how Dad and Mum worked it out, but the scooter seemed to be shared equally between them. On rainy days, she would come and pick us up from school. However, she could only take one at a time and we took it in turns to go first. Colin was much more cautious than me and would tell Mum to slow down, so I usually got to go first, which meant she would be back quicker. 'Faster, faster!' I used to shout as she weaved the ancient scooter down the winding country lanes. On one especially stormy day our luck ran out, and as the bike skidded across the road and into a ditch the pair of us flew up over the handlebars and landed in nettles. 'Are you alive?' I heard her shout.

'I am,' I said.

'Are you hurt?' she asked.

'I don't think so,' I replied, and we both started laughing. We were covered in mud and the poor old scooter was upside down.

Our accident was soon followed by Dad's accident and the writing-off of the scooter. Dad was very late coming home, and Mum was getting more and more worried. I think at one point she even said a couple of Hail Marys. Me and Colin were both up when he eventually did come home and we were shocked to see the bandages around his hands and his knee. We hadn't been able to sleep for worrying if Dad was all right, and he told us all about how he had skidded and come off the scooter and how he'd been taken off to hospital.

We had to leave Lyne Place because the council were going to put a motorway through it. Our next home was to be a beautiful bungalow called Bramdene, and I loved it there best of all, even though Mum and Dad were arguing more and more.

Chapter 21

Bramdene – Almost the End of the Road

We left Lyne Place in the mid-1960s and moved into Bramdene Cottage. It was to be our last proper home together as a family of four.

Bramdene was a bungalow situated at the end of a dirt road in the small village of Thorpe, which was even more elite than Virginia Water. All of the houses were huge and detached, and Bramdene was only slightly smaller than the rest of them. It only had two bedrooms, but they were massive, and the huge lounge really was a lounge – I remember 'lounge' being one of Mum's favourite words for a while and she was always telling people about ours, that it was a 'real' one.

The bungalow was built in a giant L-shape and it was white with bright-blue trimmings and roses growing up the walls. It was the very end house in Rosemary Lane, and it was set back from the road with a large, gravelled driveway and a garage at the side. The massive lawn had a pond and a rockery, and the garden was enclosed by fruit trees. Behind them were a wooded forest and fields.

We all loved Bramdene instantly, Mum especially, as she was sick of that 'big long fecking walk to get to anywhere'.

Soon everyone knew Mum, or knew of her; she was always the talk of the neighbourhood. Whenever she walked down the road, curtains would twitch and neighbours used to come out to their front gardens and pretend to natter over the fence so they could see what she was up to. When she wasn't talking about people, she was having rows with them. They used to whisper when she went by, and sometimes the braver ones used to say good morning or good afternoon when they wanted the latest bit of juicy gossip. She never cared what she said. When she wasn't pretending to be posh, she would always be swearing and saying terrible things to people, and Colin and I used to have to try to change the subject quickly. She had a terrible row with the local shopkeeper and she told him that his bread was at least three days old and he was a swindling old bastard. He would grovel around her after that and always give her the best groceries that he kept behind the counter out of sight of the riff-raff. Mrs Price didn't speak to her for months, though, when Mum told her that her moustache was making her look like George Harrison.

Everyone spoke about the time she got my teacher by the throat. I had been late getting to my desk one morning, and the teacher was hurrying me along and shouting at me. By the time I had got to my desk and lifted up the lid, my teacher, Miss Green*, was so angry that she hit me across the back of the head. I don't think she had intended to hurt me so badly, but the timing of her whack and my lifting the lid of my desk meant that my forehead crashed straight into the edge of the lid and split from side to side, so there was blood everywhere.

'Go and get her mother, go and get her mother!' Miss Green shouted in panic, pulling the hanky from out of her sleeve to stem the blood.

'Linda's mother will kill ya,' said one of the lads as an assortment of kids went rushing out the door and down the lane to tell my mother that I had been fatally injured.

By now I was sitting on a chair with Miss Green holding hanky after hanky to my head, all being proffered by the assembled crowd of headmistress, other teachers and any kid that could get a look-in. 'She's coming,' I heard one of the bigger kids roar, and I jumped up from the chair and looked out of the window. And there she was at the head of a huge crowd of kids and adults fighting to keep up and walk alongside her as she headed towards my school with murder on her mind. I really just wanted a cuddle from her, but I knew what she was like in that mood, and I felt sorry for Miss Green, because she honestly hadn't intended to hurt me that badly. I knew there wouldn't be any point in talking to Mum because she was stomping, not walking, and when she was stomping there was always a whack at the end of it. My poor bleeding head was quickly abandoned because everyone wanted to watch the show that was about to unfold and deserted me to find a bird's-eye view.

It wasn't much of a fight, really, but I do think my mum managed to grab Miss Green by the throat at one point. I don't remember going home and never saw any sign of an ambulance or doctor's surgery, but I do remember sitting in my bed for a couple of days with every comic I could think of and a bottle of Lucozade that Colin wasn't allowed to touch. I stayed in bed as long as I was able to, but I think I only managed about a day, long enough for all the neighbours to visit, ask about my poor head and tell Mum how amazing she was. The neighbours used to pretend to each other that they couldn't stand Mum and only used to pop in for a bit of gossip, but they always used to stay and end up giggling and singing along to the record player while we kids played and got up to anything we wanted.

Our life was never dull. Televisions and furniture would be delivered from Harrods, and Dad would send them back. Unbeknown to dad, when we were at our poorest, the three of us, me, Mum and Colin, would get dressed up in our finery and off we would go 'to see the Wizard of Oz', hopping on trains and travelling up to London to see all the sights. And we always had finery. Without my dad's knowledge, Mum had signed herself up for an account at every clothing shop within a 50-mile radius. 'Don't tell Dad,' she would whisper. And when the men used to come along to take the clothes and tellies back, she would wave her fist at them and shout, 'They were no fecking good anyway, you thieving bastards.' I think that was just in case any of the neighbours were watching. My dad would get very angry. I think he was nervous too, because he never knew what he would come home to.

I had made best friends with a kid called Sarah Atkins*. She lived really close to me, a few houses up on the right-hand side. Her house was a real mansion! Set back from the road, it backed on to acres of fields and the huge frontage was always filled with sports cars and Minis. I was so impressed with Sarah's mum because she was the only woman I had ever met who could drive. She drove Sarah to all sorts of places, and when she would allow me I would tag along. She had a little red Mini, and she would push the front seat forwards so I could climb in the back. She was a really careful and nervous driver. Actually, she drove dead slow: sometimes Sarah and I would wait at the top of the road for her coming home from work, then race her to the house, and it was usually us that got there first. I loved going in Sarah's dad's car the best, though. He had a big shiny Jaguar that was named after a big wild cat that could run really fast, and he drove like a lunatic. I loved it when he made the car jump in the air going over hills and screech going around corners. I don't think Sarah liked it very much, though, because she always looked scared, and one time she cried.

As well as being one of my closest neighbours, Sarah was in the same class as me at school, and I loved her company. We were the same age but had totally different builds: Sarah was as stout as I was thin. But we connected and bonded and became best friends. I always wanted to play at her house, because she had so much, like a paddock with her own stable and horses. I used to have to drag her down to the stables and the tackle barn, promising her it would be a laugh, because I was dying to sit up on a saddle and play pretend horse riding. We only used to sit on the saddles in the stalls and pretend to ride; at least, that was all I ever had the chance to do.

Sarah much preferred coming to my house for some reason. There were no rules. No bedtimes, no mealtimes, no structure. My mother by this time had half moved out. She was visiting and staying over, but then she would disappear again only to reappear with her latest man. I, of course, had no idea how it was breaking my poor dad's heart; he always did his best to keep it away from us. But when she did come home they would be rowing long into the night, and Colin and I would lie in bed scared, because we could hear Dad swear and he never, ever swore in front of women or children.

To me, the men were just friends of my mum and I accepted them without any qualms whatsoever. My mum and dad had made some kind of pact where they would never say anything bad about each other to me or Colin. To me, Mum and her men were just friends in the most innocent way, like me and my friend Sarah.

Out of all of Mum's friends, I liked Dennis and his three sons best. He was a huge, muscle-bound man, like the ones from the country-and-western songs Mum used to play all the time. He owned a haulage yard and drove lorries, like the man in the song 'King of the Road'. Sometimes he would drive one of his big articulated lorries down Rosemary Lane and all the neighbours would come out and stand at the front gates to take a look. Rosemary Lane was unpaved and very narrow, and Bramdene was at the very end of it, so it always caused a big stir. Mum didn't care: she would climb up the giant steps of his cab in her miniskirt and high heels, with him giving her a shove from behind. Then she would sit in the cab alongside him, backcombing her hair again to get it even higher. I don't know why she did that, because she had thick 'Paddy hair' that was twice the size of everybody else's anyway. Then they would drive off down the road with her giving a V-sign to the nosy old biddies who lined the road.

Mum used to spend ages backcombing her hair. The secret was in the amount of hairspray, she used to say, and when her hair was standing on end like she had just seen Frankenstein's monster, she would squirt it all over with hairspray from a little plastic bottle that she would squeeze until she got the very last drop out and the wind in the bottle made pump noises. 'Now get out of the way,' she would say, and I would jump quickly, because the hairspray stung my eyes and made me cough. She would smooth the top bits of her hair and hold it all in place with hundreds of hairclips. In between, she would spit on her block of mascara and then jiggle the little brush in it and add more and more coats to her eyelashes. She would then carefully draw a black line along her eyelids with a little flick at the end, like Elizabeth Taylor in *Cleopatra*. And she looked just like Cleopatra to me, with her dark hair and eyes. She was beautiful.

I loved watching Mum getting ready to go out, but she used to tell me if I touched her make-up she would throttle me and I was to keep my mitts off. Sometimes, when she was out, I would sneak into her bedroom and play with all the stuff in her top drawer and put her make-up on myself. She would always catch me, though, because the red lipstick would stain my lips and no matter how much I scrubbed them before she came home I could never get it off. I used to keep my hand over my mouth, but I would get so carried away chatting to her that I would forget to cover my lips, and then she would chase me round the house threatening me with the back of her hairbrush, saying, 'I'll murder you, you little fecker.' She didn't really mean it, though, because when she did catch me, we would end up in a bundle on the floor, giggling, and Colin would jump on top and join in.

Dad didn't like Dennis, or his big lorry, and he was scared that Mum would take me and Colin away with her and Dennis. He used to tell us that when he was drinking whisky and would get all tearful. To cheer him up, Colin and I would get him to sing us songs about the little boy that Santa Claus forgot, or the one about the wee house, but he could never remember the words to that one without crying. We couldn't understand why it made him sadder, because he loved singing.

To make Dad happy, Colin and I devised a plan to run away and hide if Mum and Dennis came down the road in the lorry. We spent a whole afternoon working on it, so we could surprise Dad when he came home. We set up an alarm system with all the kids from the village green all the way down to Rosemary Lane. By cutting through the woods and the fields and the lanes, each kid would run as fast as they could to the next messenger and pass on a warning so it would reach us before the lorry got to our house. Once the alarm reached us, Colin and I would put the second part of our plan into action.

Our bungalow had polished wooden floors that were great to slide about on, so we arranged to leave a blanket on the floor in the hall that we could jump on and slide through to the bedroom. We had pushed Colin's bed right up to the window so that we could climb out and get down onto a chair that we had left outside, and then we would run into the woods at the back of us. To be honest, the sliding bit didn't really make our escape any quicker, and even putting loads of Mum's wax on the floor to make it more slippery wasn't much help either. In most of our trial runs, we just crashed into the wall. Colin insisted that the blanket on the floor would stay, though, because it was his plan, and he was older and he was the boss.

Dad laughed his head off when we showed him how we would stop Mum taking us, and he started acting like his old self again, even though when he was scrubbing us in the bath or cooking us a meal or getting us off to school he used to mutter under his breath that a man shouldn't have to do this. He used to look really worried and then change his face, if he caught us looking at him, to make out that everything was all right.

Sometimes Mum didn't come home at all, and Dad would get really angry and tetchy and pace up and down, saying, 'Jeesy peeps, what am I going to do, what I am going to do?' I hated to see him unhappy, and when he did sit down I would climb up on his knee and give him a cuddle. When he was trying to have a snooze in his chair, I would ask him if I could do his hair, and he would always let me. I really used to want to do Mum's hair, but she would tell me to 'feck off and annoy Dad' instead. Dad never minded, and his hair was easy to comb because he always had loads of Brylcreem in it and the top part of his hair was longer so that he could comb it back when he did his quiff. I liked the long bits because I could put ribbons in it. I asked him once if his hair was tartan, because he had told me tartan was 'all different colours', and he roared with laughter and said, 'Yes, I have tartan hair.'

The saddest I saw him was when Nitty Norah came to our school. We all had to line up, then go into the medical room one by one so she could shine a lamp on our heads and look through our hair for nits. I was delighted when she told me I had nits. I always wanted things that the other kids didn't have. I didn't really know what nits were, so I asked them. Nitty Norah was talking to my teacher and the school secretary, and all three of them were tutting and looking down, shaking their heads. 'What a terrible shame,' I heard my teacher say.

'Well, you know what's going on there, don't you?' I heard the secretary say, and they all huddled in the corner, looking over at me and whispering.

'They are fleas,' my teacher finally answered, 'all jumping about on your head.'

'Tiny insects,' the secretary added. This was getting better and better. Me and Sarah Atkins loved insects, and I had a whole head full of them! I couldn't wait to tell her and Colin and everyone.

When we came out of school, Sarah and I were really excited. 'Who shall we tell first?' I asked her. I was quite happy to sit still so all the kids could sift through my hair to see if they could spot any jumping around. 'Pull my hair again and Colin'll get ya!' I yelled at the rough ones, thoroughly enjoying all the attention and knowing that my big brother would bash them if they hurt me.

Next we went off to see the woman in the local shop, thinking a bit of news like that would be bound to get us a couple of free sweets, but she just told us to clear off. The egg man thought it was a grand story, but he told me not to tell anyone else or 'me mam would skelp me'. He was an Irishman who lived in Rosemary Lane and kept loads of chickens and delivered eggs all around the area. Sometimes he would let us go with him and knock on doors and he would give us a couple of bob if we sold any.

I couldn't wait to tell Sarah's mum. She was a small, skinny, nervous woman who was easy to shock. I was always trying to think up outrageous things to say, just so that I could see the look on her face. We ran into Sarah's kitchen and her mum was standing there ironing and looking miserable as usual. 'Linda's got fleas, Linda's got fleas,' Sarah blurted out. I felt like thumping her because it was *my* news, but I just stood there scratching my head and looking smug.

'Out, out, out!' Mrs Atkins yelled, as she shooed me out the door. 'And get upstairs!' she yelled at Sarah. I wasn't expecting that reaction at all, and I was confused. As I walked away from their house, I heard Sarah calling me from her bedroom window.

'I'll meet you at the camp in a minute.'

Some of the older kids had made a camp in the woods. They had found some bits of old carpet and an old sofa that they had dragged into a small clearing. They said Sarah and I weren't allowed to use it, but we did anyway, because we could always hide when we heard them coming. As I lay down on the smelly old sofa waiting for Sarah, I wondered why all the grown-ups were acting so strangely, and I wasn't sure that having fleas was such a good thing after all.

When we got back to my house, Dad was home and Mrs Atkins was giving him a bottle of Vosene and a bottle of nit lotion from the chemist. 'You'll have to cut her hair and then put this on overnight,' I heard her say. Dad was very quiet and was speaking softly and apologetically to her, and he was looking at me with an expression of terrible disappointment. It hurt me to the core. After Mrs Atkins left with Sarah, he started shouting. I had never seen him so angry.

'Jesus,' he said, 'what am I going to do?' He was banging his fist down on the table, and he kicked the chair so hard it flew across the room. 'Who have you told? Who have you told?' he yelled at me. Of course, Colin piped up, 'She told everyone, Dad. You know what a big gob she's got.' I hated Colin at that moment – I knew he was great at lying, so why did he have to choose that moment to tell the truth? I was going to get him for that.

Then Dad went off to his room and shut the door. We knew he was really upset, so we kept really quiet, then we listened outside his door and could hear his sobs. Then Colin kicked me and ran off to the woods on his own, so I just sat there. I had hurt my dad, and he was crying. I had never seen Dad cry, or any man, and I didn't know what to do. I honestly thought my heart was going to break, but I couldn't cry.

I searched in the cabinet until I found the scissors, and I pulled a chair into the bathroom so I could see in the mirror. The first big chunk of hair I cut off was the hardest, then it got easier and easier, but I just couldn't get it straight, and there were bits standing on end. I looked funny, but I quite liked it, and I hated brushing my hair anyway.

I knocked on Dad's door gently and waited for his reply. I so wanted to make him feel better, and I said, 'Sorry, Dad,' as I walked in. I will never forget the look on his face as I walked into the room. It was a mixture of shock and horror with a desperate attempt to stifle a laugh. I started laughing, too, and ran at him and threw my arms around his neck and squeezed him tightly.

'You poor wee thing, you need a mother,' he said as he scooped me up. Colin thought my hair was hilarious, too, and as Dad sat me on the kitchen table with a bowl on my head, he kept pointing out stray bits for Dad to cut off, while we both pulled faces at each other.

I remember at Bramdene how saddened he was that he could not take care of us, and how difficult it was for fathers at that time. He was a man's man and had no idea how to take care of young children: that was a 'woman's thing', a mother's job. I quickly learned to dress myself after everyone laughed at my cross-over skirt because he had put it on me back to front.

Only now can I imagine how troubled he must have been. He worked long, gruelling hours and had two small children to look after. He wrote to my grandmother and, soon after, one of our older cousins arrived on the doorstep. Agnes* was the daughter of Moira*, one of my mum's older sisters. She stayed with us for a few weeks, but she quickly became best pals with Mum, who was not much older than her, and their joint antics left us pretty much in the same position as before as far as childcare was concerned. I believe Dad must have reached the end of his tether, because he took the bold decision to send the pair of us back to Ireland with Agnes. He believed that we would be better off in the care of our aunt and grandmother in Ireland, and he sent us off, heartbroken but totally convinced he had done the right thing for our well-being.

* * *

Reliving those childhood memories, I felt as though this court case had become a battle for my mind. In the past, I would have been among the first to condemn my mother, and for that I am deeply ashamed now. I couldn't help but blame her for the break-up of our family, the estrangements, the lunatic decisions I had made throughout my life. It was her fault I had never been happy – or normal. After all, it is almost always the mother to blame – or so most people say. I told people I didn't have a mother, or that I did but that she was bonkers if I wanted to put them off. She was a secret I shared only with those closest to me.

But the court case had made me think, and think deeply. The more Omni degraded and cast aspersions on my mother and my father, the more compelled I felt to defend them. They were both now gone, and I had never loved them more.

The good memories were fighting the bad memories in my head. I was in turmoil. I felt a blinding flash, a crazy realisation that I had allowed the bad memories to dominate my life. It made no sense, and I wondered how I could have been so stupid. The only person denying me happiness was me.

I felt as though I was finally finding the answers to the questions that had haunted me all my life. I suddenly realised why I could never get along with Freud. Why the need to drag out the trauma of childhood? Why do we need to face up to it? Why should a rape victim have to relive the horror again and again? I have never heard of any good that has come of it. Why don't psychologists focus on the happy memories? They give you strength; they give you that all-elusive contentment that doesn't come out of a bottle or from a drug. It's not all tragedy. Everybody laughs sometimes.

In my battle to hang on to my sanity during the whole court ordeal, I needed to dig into my past, I needed to find that strong, cocky little kid who brimmed with confidence, the one who had existed before I had gone into the convent.

Over and over, the phrase 'you used to be a happy child' haunted me. If I was a happy child when I arrived at the convent, then any damage must have occurred there. Surely that proved my case, not the defendants'? 'Give me the child until he is seven and I will give you the man' – isn't that the accepted wisdom? I remember reading that a child who is given enough love will never grow up to be a criminal, and it is true in my case: neither I nor my brother – nor any member of our family – grew up to be a criminal. Those words became words of wisdom for a reason.

How dare Omni say my mother had never loved me; he never knew her. In my mind, I could see her hovering in the clouds, rolling up her sleeves and screaming, 'Let me at him!'

I could see Dad, too, a tear rolling down his cheek with pride. His greatest joy was my and my brother's achievements and our kids. 'Och, there's nothing to it,' I could hear him say, and I could imagine him giving me a shove as I stepped into the witness box. He always told me things were easy even if they weren't, and because he believed in me he persuaded me to believe in myself, too. I left him to nudge his pals and make sure they were listening as he took a ringside seat, sitting forward with his arms folded but constantly at the ready to point out the good bits, in case anyone missed them. Yeah, both of them were there with me, and I had a battle to fight.

Day Two

Chapter 22

Psychologists' Evidence

Despite all our precautions, Lynn and I overslept the following morning. I glanced at the clock that said twenty to nine and screamed in panic. I was due at the court at 9 a.m. I had less than twenty minutes in which to shower, apply make-up and run to the court. On top of which I couldn't for the life of me remember where the building was. I was still under oath and due back in the witness box, and my solicitor had to guide me in by giving me directions via our mobile phones.

Breathless and dishevelled, I made it into the courtroom fractionally before the judge arrived. Or perhaps he had been waiting and was going to be angry. I apologised anyway and dabbed at the perspiration running down my neck as I stumbled back into the witness box. The judge reminded me that I was still under oath and that they would pick up from where they had left off.

Omni seemed to be looking forward to coming in for the kill. He had landed some knockout blows. I had been a happy child. The documents in front of all of us confirmed it. It was written there in black and white. Omni took a moment to stand back and enjoy his victory. And I knew that I had been a happy child. My memories of my early childhood were good memories, and they were my memories. What had happened to distort them, to change them?

Omni changed his line of questioning and barked at me again, 'Your mother rejected you, did she not?'

'No,' I insisted.

'Just answer the question,' he said impatiently.

The judge intervened and said I had answered the question: I had said, 'No.'

The barrister tried putting it another way. 'I am merely trying to establish that if Miss Hutton has suffered any psychological damage, it was caused prior to her entering St Anne's Convent. It is a valid line of questioning, Your Honour.'

The judge looked down at his papers, shuffled them around a bit and then nodded for him to carry on.

'So I ask you again, do you honestly believe that you should be compensated for being called Madam Hutton?' Omni scoffed.

'It was more than name-calling,' I replied, 'so much more.'

Omni rocked back and forth on his heels for a few moments and rubbed his chin as he thought up his next line. 'You are a very bitter woman, aren't you, Miss Hutton?'

'No, I am not bitter, I am angry.' I had rehearsed this speech many times over in my head for almost five years. I had lived, and relived, every awful event that I had been witness to and victim of. I knew everything that I wanted to say; it had played over and over in my head for so long. I knew it so well, but I hadn't taken into account the fact that my emotions might spill over, or that the stifling atmosphere of the courtroom and the gruelling questions would reduce me to a blubbering heap. That wasn't what I had envisaged at all.

'Would you like a recess, Miss Hutton?' the judge asked kindly. 'A few moments to compose yourself?'

I didn't know what to do. I wanted it to stop, but I also wanted to speak. This was my moment, maybe even the only opportunity I would ever have to tell my story. I was still under oath, and I had to tell them, I had to tell the stories that I had saved up in my head for all those years, the stories that haunted me and had blighted so much of my adult life. Why was I crippled with depression? Why couldn't I fall in love, like other people? Why couldn't I trust anyone? Why was I angry? Why was I always getting the sack? Why couldn't I keep my big mouth shut?

My own psychologist, Joanna, was the first witness to be called after me. A larger-than-life character, Joanna stood out from every other person in the courtroom in her brightly coloured suit, like a prim, softer, yet somehow more rebellious version of the house-cleaning Kim from *How Clean Is Your House?*. As she stood in the witness box, I noticed that the bright colour of her chic suit and queenly pearls softened the formality of her academic credentials and set her apart from the other professionals.

I think Joanna is probably the most honest person I have ever met, almost brutally so. I doubt many people have read such in-depth psychological profiles of themselves as I have. Who would want to? It is bad enough examining one's own mind without having a professional do it. And not one professional did I have, but two: one giving evidence for my side and one giving evidence for the Catholic Church.

Omni started off with questions on the points the psychologists agreed on. They both agreed that I was of good character and that they had no reason to believe that I was lying. I was pleased about that.

Joanna argued that the social worker's notes referred to my brother and me as bright and happy children when she delivered us to the convent. Miss Bradshaw had delivered two bright, cheerful and well-adjusted children to the nuns: the documentation supported that. But the documents described, too, the changes to me that had occurred within the convent, as stated by the written reports of Sister Consolata and Peter Rands: 'Linda is sulky'; 'Linda is petulant'; 'Linda has developed an arrogance that is extremely unattractive'. I was angered by their words. Yes, I had withdrawn into myself, I had taken my very own vow of silence, but I had had my reasons. It had become the only way to survive. The psychological damage (I was not so pleased about that), Joanna asserted, had been caused by my time at St Anne's.

Then she referred to my disassociation, my multiple personalities. 'And you witnessed it here yourselves,' she informed the court.

I sat at the back of the court, cringing yet narcissistic enough to want to hear every word she said. I was half starting to believe that what she said might even be true. I could not remember giving evidence the day before – or, rather, I remembered the words, but I didn't remember 'me' saying them. Maybe there was another me – a better one?

'There was an actual physical transformation,' Joanna said. 'We all saw it here yesterday. That cannot be faked.' She then went on to explain that you cannot fake the dilation of your pupils or a change in the colour of your skin. Apparently, as I had answered questions about the convent I had visibly paled before their eyes.

As much as I respected Joanna, I was still sceptical. I didn't truly believe that I had been damaged or that I had developed multiple personalities – as much as I loved the drama of it. 'It was just the way things were in those days' was a phrase that I repeated over and over to myself. It was true that I had, on the whole, wrecked my life, and it was nobody's fault but my own. Yet Joanna told me that I still didn't know, that I still didn't understand just how deeply the awful experiences of the convent had affected me. And she said it almost guiltily, as though she knew in her heart that trials such as these stir up demons from the past that can prove fatal. Very few people can survive. And if you lose, there is nothing and no one there to pick up the pieces.

Joanna had told me before we went into the courtroom that I was bright and that was the reason I had survived, and she told me that my father was an amazing man. She told me the things I really needed to hear. Perhaps she did understand me after all. Perhaps she was right, perhaps I did not need to hate myself quite as much as I did. Joanna understood that my dad had been my rock and that I had fallen apart when he died.

She didn't mention my mother, and I didn't blame her for that. Mothers are a touchy area in psychology, but I had forgiven my mother many years before and we had been reconciled. And as the years went by, the word 'forgive' seemed pompous and ridiculous. My mum was what she was, and I began to find her eccentricity endearing, in the way so many other people had. I was shocked to discover that she had good friends who adored her and relieved to find that she hadn't robbed any banks or murdered anyone during the years we were estranged. Of course, she was still a terrible woman, but I loved her anyway.

Joanna was confident in the witness box, much more confident than I had been, and even though she was polite and proper, she spoke to the judge as if he were her intellectual and social equal. There was no deference from her. She gave her evidence professionally and knowledgably, but to be honest most of it was quite technical and went right over my head.

Omni didn't change his stance at all as he reeled off questions to her, he was just as haughty and flamboyant as he had been with me, but she remained unruffled.

The psychologist for the defendants was a professor, a renowned expert in his field, with plush offices in Harley Street. He didn't look like the lawyers, either: his clothes were sort of grey, but they were scruffy, the collar of his shirt was open and he wore no tie. It was a sort of academic chic, the clothes of a man who placed knowledge above conventional attire, a man who had submitted to the letter of the law and the bibles of psychology but allowed his hair to flop into his eyes to show that he hadn't quite accepted everything.

He shuffled in the witness box as he gave his evidence for the defendants. He described my childhood as one of the most tragic he had ever encountered. He kept his head down, almost ashamed to look me in the eye. He agreed with Joanna that I was not a liar, and he agreed with Joanna that I disassociated: how could he not? I squirmed in my seat, still refusing to accept that these two experts could know more about myself than I did.

Listening to two psychologists giving for and against arguments about you is right up there with life's most bizarre experiences, akin to seeing aliens, I would think. I was glad that I couldn't understand most of it. They went off into using all sorts of psychological terms and describing experiments and even *moi*, the possible new founder of Narcissists Anonymous, switched off.

The gloom of the court was getting to me, and the sad times were flooding my mind along with the good. I felt as though I were undergoing some freaky form of psychological torture in Room 101. My entire childhood was being dissected, spit-roasted and then eaten as sandwiches the next day. I had no option but to raid and torment my troubled mind further, searching for answers in the past, wanting the truth confirmed. For if it was not, then surely I was mad?

I suffered mentally when I was at the convent. I was at the point of suicide when I started my periods because I was running out of ways to hide it and of ways to get, and then get rid of, sanitary towels. I had a plastic bag full of them under my bed, and I prayed every night that the good Lord would strike me dead if I got found out. I was reading a lot of the Brontë sisters' stuff at the time and martyrdom seemed the only way out. I became very pensive and quiet for ages as I toyed with ways in which to kill myself. On the practical side, throwing myself under a double-decker bus seemed to be the best option, but it would be a bit squishy, and I wanted to look beautiful in my coffin: the more gorgeous I looked, the worse the nuns would feel over what they had done to me.

Not that anyone ever actually noticed I was on the brink of suicide – sometimes I really felt like doing it, just to show them that I meant it! I absolutely loved that particular fantasy. Following my demise, Sister Consolata would have to stand in front of a court of her own peers and tell them what an evil cow she was and how holy and saintly I was. That bit would kill her.

My death scenarios took me away for hours on end in my head and always involved some evil scheme based around revenge. I am not sure that I actually wanted to die, although I had rehearsed my death scene in my mind over and over. It would be long and drawn out, like Cathy's in *Wuthering Heights*, so I would have time to tell everyone what I thought of them. Then I thought I would make myself look even holier by forgiving them before I drew my last breath, so they would feel even worse. And I didn't really feel guilty about it, because I could always go to confession.

The nun used to say I was walking around like a martyr to get everyone's attention and would mock me and get the others to join in and laugh when she said, 'Look at the gob on Madam Hutton!' I knew all the saints and martyrs had been abused on an almost daily basis, so I tried to resign myself to it and went further and further into reading any book I could get hold of.

I wanted so much to smash my fist into Sister Consolata's fat, round, smug face. I hated her so much that I cried myself to sleep so many nights, my head buried under the pillow and the covers so that no one could hear.

I had entered into a phase of 'dumb insolence'. I no longer answered the nun back or reacted to her jibes and spite. I did my chores quickly and efficiently, and I disappeared for hours on end, my head buried in a book. I sat under trees, even in the rain, and read and read until the fading light prevented me from reading any more. As I did my chores, I took my mind away to another world, a world where everything was different and where I would never see a hated nun again.

Chapter 23

It Couldn't Have Been All Bad

Back in the courtroom, Omni was continuing with his mind games. 'Your memories of St Anne's couldn't have been *all* bad,' he said. He was referring to the later years, when the nuns had moved out. 'It says here that you and Colin complained to Miss Bradshaw that you had to go to bed early, that you were not allowed to stay up to watch television.' And it was true. We had. But I couldn't get him to understand the difference. At the time we had complained, Uncle Peter and Sister Consolata were gone. A sane woman had been put in charge of Don Bosco: Aunty Mary, a normal person who genuinely cared for the children in care. Aunty Mary was a middle-aged lady who had travelled the world. Interesting and intelligent, she treated us as human beings. We children were no longer living in morbid fear of the retribution that existed when Sister Consolata and Uncle Peter were in charge of our house. Our final months at St Anne's were not unhappy; with Aunty Mary in charge we could be children again. Omni was referring to those end days, trying to blur the issues, sweeping away the previous horrors as if they had never existed.

Omni was prompting me for an answer, swirling his deathly white hand in the air to add pizzazz and beckoning with his fingertips for my reply. Perhaps he thought that he could appeal to the last remnants of Catholicism I might have left inside me. Perhaps he was hoping I would tell him a story about a kindly nun who had stepped forward and screamed, 'Stop all this madness!' I didn't have one. Not one person in authority had ever intervened.

No, my memories were not all bad. I had friends that I loved dearly, friends who truly knew what it was to help out a mate. We had shared an awful experience that only others who had lived it would understand. I did have good memories from the convent. In the face of the enemy, there was a feeling of camaraderie among the kids and we helped each other out where we could. But we were so often put in situations where we were helpless to assist others, and although I cannot speak for anyone else I know that it has left me with a feeling of lasting guilt that haunts me to this day.

The convent, contrary to how it felt, was not a prison. Mole and I went to a school that was not only off the premises but two bus rides away. We went to St Bernadette's Catholic girls' school in St Mary Cray, with normal kids from normal homes. However, we were notorious, partly for our bad behaviour (we went wild when out of the nuns' sight) but mostly simply because we were convent girls. We weren't like the other pupils; we didn't come from good, respectable Catholic families.

The teachers barely tolerated us, and it felt as though the headmistress actively disliked us. Every classroom and hall had a crackly speaker on the wall where the headmistress could speak through her microphone to everyone at once. As soon as the weird noises started coming out of it, Molly, Danielle* and I would start to pack our books up before our names and the names of all the other convent girls were even announced. We always knew we were the first, and probably only, suspects for anything bad that might have occurred in or outside of the school. This usually meant detention outside of the headmistress's office, where we would all have to stand in a row until someone confessed.

Sometimes it did involve one of us, but most of the time it didn't, because we would be too busy trying to rush home to get our chores done so we could watch a bit of telly. For having detention, we would get further punishment from the nuns when we got in.

I quite liked being one of the 'convent girls' – it was like being in a gang, without really knowing at the time what a gang was. It was as if you had loads of sisters: big and small, black and white, you were family, and you looked out for each other.

Most of the convent girls were quite tough, and I wanted to be tough, too. But within the convent girls, we had our own little groups, too. I was the same age and in the same year group as Molly, Danielle and a girl called Shirley*. We stuck together all the time, laughing and giggling our way through school and the bus journeys but never knowing what new nightmare awaited us on our return.

Karen and the school nurse supplied me with sanitary towels when the inevitable happened. Karen also gave me my first two bras. My need was small, something like 28AAA, but urgent nevertheless, and the bras she gave me were beautiful: a pink and black one and a plain pink one from Dorothy Perkins.

We remained friends, despite the fact that the greatest love of my life was in love with her (I'll come to that in a minute). We had always vowed never to let a boy come between us. We even cut our fingers and mingled our blood on the playing field to seal the pact. I didn't even blame him for liking Karen, because she was without doubt the prettiest girl in our school and in the convent – and the kindest.

Being that little bit older, Karen's thoughts and attentions had turned towards boys. They all loved her, and I didn't blame them. She was gorgeous. On the other hand, I wore the worst clothes Sister Consolata could possibly find me. We had now been given funding to go 'out' and buy clothes rather than get them from the convent store, but my shopping trips with the nun were torture. She bought me skirts that were neither mini, midi or maxi, or else bought clothes with ridiculous patterns or in drab colours. I will never forget the hideous black and white checked coat she bought me. I had tears rolling down my cheeks as she told the shop assistant we would take it. On top of that, I had unruly brown hair that I couldn't be bothered to brush and not a hint of a curve in sight. I often read 'The Ugly Duckling' and consoled myself with the thought that maybe I would blossom one day.

Karen was truly an angel. She would take me up to her room and give me clothes she didn't need any more, and even some she still really liked. She would take the time to brush the knots out of my hair gently and help me to style it so I looked like a girl instead of the madwoman in the attic. I wasn't really keen on boys for a while; they were mostly annoying – apart from Philip, who was a god – they always got rough, and I wasn't enjoying punch-ups with them as much as I used to.

I was in awe of Karen and used to follow her around like an annoying little sister. She was so pretty and bright and had smiles for everyone, and everyone loved her. She was the complete opposite of me. I spoke only to my brother and my closest friends. The world was too horrible and I no longer wanted to be part of it. My summer of silence had even spilled over into our visits from Dad, and he asked me why I never smiled any more. He said I was pretty when I smiled, and I tried it out in the mirror later, but I didn't think I was. He said I used to be gregarious, too, but I didn't know what that meant, so I had to look it up in the dictionary. I couldn't remember seeking or enjoying the company of others – or if I ever did, the memory was vague and blurry.

Being sent to Coventry had tipped me over into a solitary world of books and thoughts that I couldn't come back from, even long after the punishment was over. People were talking to me again, but I couldn't always respond. My silence was taken for arrogance or dumb insolence and the punishments increased, but I didn't care, because they couldn't hurt me any more: in my head, I could escape.

Karen brought me back to reality. For her, I was willing to put my book down and chatter and sometimes even giggle again, and our favourite topic of conversation became boys.

Michael Glancy* had come to the convent and moved into the house next door, and I truly thought I was going to die from being lovestruck and smitten. Michael was 14, the same age as Karen, and he was tall and tanned with blonde hair and a big nose. He was of

Greek origin, or maybe Maltese. I didn't care about his big conk – I loved that too! I used to blush and go all silly and girly in his presence and do and say everything wrong – when I was able to talk, that is, because when he looked at me I usually lost the power of speech.

He was always around at Don Bosco. Sometimes he would come out in the garden with us, and I would wind him up so that he would play-fight with me, and we would end up on the ground, almost kissing. I couldn't eat, I couldn't sleep, I couldn't concentrate on my books for thinking about him, and I couldn't wait to tell Karen.

Karen knew all about unrequited love: she was in love with my brother, Colin! I couldn't see what she saw in him myself, but I was happy to listen to her gibbering on about him, so I could gibber on about Michael. Sadly, for me, Michael was in love with Karen, but happily for me, Karen was in love with Colin. And thus began our tragic little love triangle, or perhaps that should have been a love square, or a love pentagon if you counted the irritating little fat kid who followed me around.

Michael only liked me if Karen wasn't around, but the moment she entered the room or came into the garden I was quickly forgotten, and he would find excuses to play-fight with her. She always assured me that it never meant anything to her and that her heart was elsewhere, but Michael followed her around like a lovesick puppy and I read novels that confirmed, yes, it was absolutely true you could die of a broken heart. The only good thing was you could come back and haunt the person who had spurned you by tapping on their window during the night so that they would know what they had lost. I had just read *Wuthering Heights*.

It was 1971, and as Mole and I were only weeks apart with our birthdays, we were allowed to have a joint party in the playroom and invite some friends from the other houses. It was a first, and a sign that things were changing within the convent. Aunty Molly had requested it, as we were both becoming teenagers. We were so excited because we had managed to buy a whole album of hit songs. Well, an LP from Woolworths anyway. It wasn't very good because the songs weren't performed by the real artists, but it had 'Chirpy Chirpy

Cheep Cheep' on it. Happily we were allowed to put the radio on for the Top 20 countdown on Radio 1, so we had some decent music. I kept hoping that Michael would ask me to dance to Hurricane Smith's 'Don't Let It Die', which was my absolute favourite song, and in my imagination, when it played it would be the moment that Michael finally realised that he did love me after all.

The whole party was a hotbed of adolescent hormones and unrequited love. When Karen brushed Michael off to make a beeline for Colin, Michael put 'Hey Girl Don't Bother Me' on the record player and dedicated it to me, so I thumped the fat kid. The party ended up with everyone singing along to the song about Ernie, who drove the fastest milk cart in the west. The party hadn't turned out anything like I had planned. I felt as though my chances of ever finding love had gone for ever, my dream of Michael singing 'Don't Let It Die' as we danced close and smooched was never to be. I was destined to be an old maid. It was highly unlikely I would ever love again.

When Mum came to visit me, I asked if I could have my hair cut short like Mia Farrow or Joan of Arc, or even Twiggy, but she said only lesbians had short hair like that. She wouldn't tell me what lesbians were, other than that they were women wearing men's clothes who hung around public conveniences with their hair cut short. I wasn't sure she was telling the truth, because I had never seen them, but she wouldn't have it. She said there was no point in becoming a lesbian just because a boy I liked liked someone else.

I hadn't planned on becoming a lesbian; I just wanted to look angelic, lovelorn and mystical. I still had my Hurricane Smith record safely stored away in my bottom drawer in case Michael ever changed his mind. But, in fairness, I had started noticing little faults in him that I had been blind to before. He really did have one hell of a big hooter on him, and if he ever did kiss me it was bound to get in the way. His teeth were quite large, too, and I didn't have a clue what happened to teeth and noses while you were snogging, because I had never been kissed before, and now it was never going to happen.

I even discussed my future spinsterhood with one of my best

185

friends at school. Her name was Lorraine and she loved the same books as me. She too had experienced lost love. Hers was a boy called Steve who worked in the butcher's in Orpington High Street and who had failed to notice her despite the number of excuses she found to go in there and see him.

We accepted our fate: we were destined to become governesses or Miss Marples, dedicating our lives to art and music and writing, so that nobody would know that we had really been left on the shelf. Being left on the shelf was just about the worst thing that could ever happen to a girl, but I didn't feel so bad, knowing that Lorraine was going to be an old maid too. It sort of made the pain more bearable.

We had taken up the cause of the Cherokee Indians and were wearing our hair in plaits to support them. *Soldier Blue* was the big film of the day, and although we weren't old enough to go and see it – because it was a bloodbath, apparently – we knew enough about the cause to feel affronted. Besides, we loved Buffy Sainte-Marie, who had recorded the film's theme song, as well as fellow supporter of the cause Marlon Brando; they seemed to be troubled souls just like ourselves.

One of the first records I ever bought was a six-inch vinyl disc, 'Vincent' by Don McLean, a song dedicated to the tragic artist Vincent Van Gogh, who had been so heartbroken that he had cut his ear off. I had recently seen the Kirk Douglas film about his life, so I knew all about him. I knew exactly how Vincent felt, crazy in love, but not sure with who or what.

I played the record over and over in my new-found friend Danielle's house, Holy Family. Her house had recently got a new nun, and they were now allowed visitors and they also had a record player in their waiting room that the kids were allowed to use. Danielle had an older sister, Dawn*, who was very scholarly and religious, and she didn't like me at all. She thought I was a bad influence on her little sister. As the nuns started to move back into the main convent, we were given more freedoms, one of which was to join the Girl Guides. Karen had been a pack leader for ages, because her nun had allowed her to join the Guides long before the girls in the other houses, and I was dead proud that she was my friend.

Chapter 24

The Penguins Are Coming!

After the move to Don Bosco, we got to know more of the other kids at the convent. We had seen each other so often at church, and even sometimes during the school holidays, when we were allowed into the playground. Some, of course, we knew from school.

Once a year, almost the entire convent would pack up and head to the seaside. The holidays were a time to look forward to. Excitement filled the air in the weeks leading up to it. The first holiday I remember was our two weeks in Dymchurch. It was an annual thing, and most of the other kids knew the routine. It was an exciting time as we packed up the cases to go. Molly and I had to get all the holiday clothes out of storage and then help Sister Consolata to sort out who was going to take what for each of the kids.

The holiday clothes were years old and had been worn by many generations before us for the annual holiday to Dymchurch, but we didn't care. However, I was devastated at first to have been given a blue bubble swimsuit like the little kids wore, especially as it was one of those ones where all the bubbles filled with water and dragged the costume down, showing your nipples. Happily, I was physically immature and the thought of jumping into the sea filled me with glee. I didn't care if I had to spend the day pulling the swimsuit up.

I had no memory of having gone to the seaside before, and Molly and Karen were happy to tell me all the details, over and over again. And I wasn't disappointed. We did indeed sleep in dormitories with rows of wooden bunk beds, like the prisoner-of-war camps in the old films. And we had grey pillows with black stripes, and the feathers poked through and scratched your face. The blankets were dirty grey, too, and every bed had meticulous hospital corners where the blankets were tucked in. We all ran in, laughing and chatting, baggsying our beds. Me and Molly shared a bunk bed and took it in turns to have the top and bottom, using our guile to confuse the nuns.

Everyone loved going on holiday – even the mood of the nuns lifted. We were always first on the beach because we would arrive at the crack of dawn – holidays, sadly, did not include a lie-in. Not that we minded, the excitement was enough. The nuns used to sit in the deckchairs dressed in their full regalia, shielded by a row of brightly coloured, stripy windbreakers, drinking tea out of flasks and telling us to clear off. Sometimes strangers would go up to them and give them pound notes and tell them to buy all the kids an ice cream. And we got them, too, probably because there were too many witnesses around for the nuns not to buy them, or because the donor would always come back at some point to get their gracious thanks from all the orphans. Being an object of pity didn't really bother me, because we got loads of treats.

The only bits of the nuns that could get the sun were their faces and the backs of their hands, and a few of them rolled their sleeves up, or at least the younger ones did. It got very confusing with Sister Consolata, however, because we usually used the colour of her face to gauge how mad she was – bright red being the signal to run. When she smiled and was sunburned, she looked demented.

We had to get changed on the beach, but it was OK because you had to put your swimsuit on instead of your vest and pants, so you just had to slip your clothes and shoes off when you got there. Getting dressed to come home was horrible, though. The towels were shared, and the only privacy you could get was by putting two windbreakers together, but the boys would act the goat and keep pulling them down to annoy you.

We would have our lunch on the beach. The catering people would load us up each morning with hundreds of packs of ham or cheese sandwiches wrapped in greaseproof paper. The sandwiches were horrible and sometimes they even had icy bits in the middle where they were still defrosting. The little ones always used to drop theirs in the sand, but a nun would make them eat them anyway and it used to make me feel sick.

After lunch, we would return to the dormitories, supposedly to sleep, while the nuns all went off to prayer. This was a time of joy that we all looked forward to, every house from the entire convent. Every nun would go, leaving not a single guard to keep an eye on us. We could barely contain ourselves when we heard a bell and then saw them all heading off. You could hear the collective sighs of 'yes' passing through the halls. It was an hour, maybe two, of pure bliss. We were able to run up and down the dormitories like lunatics; the girls could go into the boys' dormitories and the boys could go into the girls'. Or we could simply spend precious moments speaking to our friends from the other houses.

We had a well-thought-out system in place throughout the entire Dymchurch holiday camp, and no child would live if they dared to split! Lookouts were posted every day and everyone had to take a turn, and as soon as a nun came into sight the cry would be whispered down the line until it reached its crescendo, when we all jumped back onto our bunks shouting, 'The Penguins are coming, the Penguins are coming!', stopping abruptly as the doors opened.

The nuns mellowed at Dymchurch. Some of them even seemed happy, and Sister Rebecca was busying herself organising our pantomime. Each year, the different homes would put on a show at the end of the holiday, and the afternoons were dedicated to casting it, doing the costumes and rehearsing.

I thought of Sister Rebecca as one of the younger nuns, because she seemed a bit different and she wasn't as ugly as the rest of them. Sometimes she would even have a laugh and joke with you. On one holiday, we all wanted to latch on to her as we went round the fairground, because she was the only nun who would accept the offer of a free ride and all the kids that were with her would get to go on it too.

We were putting on *Snow White and the Seven Dwarfs*. The pantomimes were a yearly opportunity for the show-off kids to release some energy and they were an opportunity for the nuns to flex their creative sides, so even they seemed to enjoy them. I am not sure how true our version was to the original, because Colin played some evil singing wizard (with relish), and I don't remember one of them in the fairy tale, and Mole was dressed up as Little Red Riding Hood. I prayed with every fibre in my body that I would get the part of Snow White. I loved singing and my granny said I had the voice of an angel. If there was any justice in the world, the part would be mine.

I promised God that I would stop swearing, I would be a good Catholic and I would even try to like Sister Consolata if I could only have the part. Of course, I had to let on to all the others that I wasn't bothered at all one way or the other and that I would be more than happy to play any part that was given to me. The truth was the opposite, of course: if I didn't get the part, the shame would surely kill me. I dragged any kid who would cooperate to one side so I could sing to them and they would hear what an angelic voice I had. I even sang when I knew Sister Rebecca was in hearing distance, so she would ask, 'Who is that child singing?' and give me the part instantly.

It didn't happen, of course. I was given the part of the wicked witch, and I had to say, 'That's fantastic,' through gritted teeth. My little heart was breaking. The part of Snow White was offered to the beautiful, blonde, cherubic Karen, and as much I loved her I had horrible pangs of jealousy. To make it even worse, she did not want the part, and so it went to her equally beautiful and cherubic little sister Rita.

My role was to come onto the stage dressed as an evil old witch in black rags and a pointy hat, singing, 'Apples are red, my love,' to the tune of 'Roses Are Red (My Love)' while enticing the celestial Snow White to have a bite of my apple.

I loved the rehearsals and the amazing singing lessons from Sister Rebecca, and Rita and I would sit outside on the grass together practising whenever we could. My biggest problem was whether to sing my song with a Patsy Cline twang or as an angelic choirboy, and we would dissolve into fits of giggles trying it out in opera and pop and all different styles.

Rita's song was a million times harder. She had to sing 'Some Day My Prince Will Come', which had bits so high even a soprano would have struggled. But she could do it, and she sounded wonderful.

When the day of our performance came, I hadn't reckoned on exactly how horrendous my costume was going to be. I was going to be absolutely humiliated, especially as Colin had somehow wangled his way into the make-up bit and thought of the great idea of sticking green plasticine onto my nose to make it look like I had warts, too. Even though I knew that I was destined to be a plain, single governess of some sort in the future, I somehow hoped that Michael would see the poor yet fascinating tortured soul behind the green warty nose and the fuzzy hair.

I had hoped the other kids, too, would see past the costume and appreciate my beautiful voice as I stepped out on stage, but, as it happened, it was a hundred times worse than I thought it would be. Not only did they boo, some were even throwing things. The nuns were hooting with laughter. I don't know what kind of reception I was expecting, but it certainly wasn't that. Despite all the booing and hissing, I hit each note perfectly, even though I could hear my voice shaking. I don't know where I got the courage from, because really I just wanted to run away and cry. I sort of felt defiant for the next couple of days, because I couldn't get the black off my eyes and I looked gorgeous like Dusty Springfield. Michael spoke to me, and he said I was great in the show. That really meant a lot.

Chapter 25

The Smoking Gun

....

I finished giving my evidence and was released from my oath, and I was free to sit beside Lynn at the back of the court and watch as witnesses were called.

My one and only witness, Rita, was due to give video evidence from Australia, and it seemed so strange that I was about to see her face to face, albeit on a screen, for the first time in almost 40 years. Rita had suffered her own abuse at St Anne's and was well aware of the way in which the homes had been run.

But Rita wasn't called, and in the confusion I gathered that her evidence had been agreed by the other side. It felt as though it should have been a devastating blow to my case, but my barrister told me not to worry, and she was smiling and looking confident. It seemed that my side had finally won a court order for the release of Peter Rands's personnel file. The legal team for the Catholic Church had fought long and hard to keep the file under wraps. Peter Rands, it seemed, had died at the end of the previous year, of cancer of the anus.

I thought about Peter Rands only occasionally now, but when I did it was with a mixture of curiosity, bewilderment and sheer horror. Although I was no longer afraid of him, I had spent a lifetime trying to understand what had made him tick, and why did he tick so differently to everyone else? I had always been looking for answers.

I had so wanted to know what Mum had meant when she first confronted him and said, 'I know what you are.' It was as if she had some kind of supreme wisdom that I would never have. At that exact moment, I had known that the adults in the room had a shared knowledge, and I wanted to know what it was.

I think I had heard people say that he had been the first uncle to go and work at St Anne's. Prior to that, the children had been cared for by the nuns and a few female lay staff who lived in. Peter Rands was the only uncle in the homes when Colin and I had first arrived there, and we who lived in Tara were the ones 'lucky' enough to have him.

My barrister said we had 'got them' as she waved the papers in the air, her gown falling off her shoulders again and again. I kept wondering why all the barristers' gowns kept falling down; it had been the same during the criminal trial at which I had been a juror. I was curious as to why they didn't get gowns to fit, or use safety pins, but the posturing was all part of the show. Reaching their arms back to retrieve their gowns leaves them with their fists on their chests, with their thumbs pointing upwards in victory. Even Deborah, my barrister, did it, but I liked it from her. She was young, beautiful and very professional, and she made her grey, black and white garb look chic and glamorous. And she was human, too, not even bothering to remove her wig when we nipped outside for a fag.

'I put it to you that this document is a smoking gun,' Deborah said confidently, back in the courtroom, as she referred the Church's trembling witness to the file in front of him. Sounding like Vicky Pollard from *Little Britain*, he squirmed and stuttered, 'Yes, but, no, but.'

The files showed that Peter Rands had been dismissed from the convent's employment and that he had also been dismissed from the boys' home where he had later worked. He had been caught with a 15-year-old boy (not any of the boys I've mentioned in this book) in his bed, yet he had never been prosecuted. He had manipulated and organised the boys in such a way that they saw him as their leader, a martyr, a sacrificial lamb who cared more for them than anyone they had ever met before. He took them to see kinky films like *The Devils*, and then held organised discussions afterwards on the merits of nuns and priests being raped. Happily, there was a lay member of staff around who finally blew the whistle. The report also revealed that Peter Rands had opened clothing accounts in Burton that he charged to his employers and that he had groomed a boy and enticed him to leave his parents. He had misappropriated funds and he had falsified records. All this, however, was not enough to earn him a conviction anywhere along the way, and Omni had admonished me for attempting to blacken Rands's character with the trial.

Everything I had said about Peter Rands was true, and the evidence was there to support it in the form of the personnel file. The defendants had tried to suppress it, but the judge had ruled against them. It was a huge victory for my side, but Rands had never been my main target, or even Sister Consolata. I had wanted to see Uncle Tim, Bimbo, on trial; I wanted to see him punished for his crimes. I felt tears of anger and frustration as I realised my own main abuser would never face a trial.

The abuser I wanted to get, the one I was really after, wasn't there, and I had waited so many years to face him. His name had been redacted, blacked out, not known by the defendants, or their servants, or their agents. But his name had been known to someone, because someone had blacked it out. And I would never know why.

Chapter 26

Across the Sea to Ireland

As the case continued, my mind was in turmoil. Maybe they were right? Maybe they had been right along? I had heard more about myself than any soul should ever know. Every belief I had ever had had been shattered and thrown out to the wind. Nothing seemed real any more, nothing seemed constant, except for Big Lynn. To her, reality was what she saw in front of her own eyes.

On our third night in the hotel room, lying on our beds, we could feel an intense sense of righteousness. Over the years, Big Lynn had become part and parcel of my 'cause', my fight for justice. She could see things as I did, and we were at odds with the world.

We lay there talking late into the night, and she was as appalled as I that these religious people had refused to give evidence or to swear an oath to their statements. We wondered how that worked. Could they count on final absolution to cleanse their souls for the next world?

Big Lynn had known much sorrow through her life. She had lost too many lovers and friends to alcohol and drugs – mostly former victims of care homes and childhood abuse. We had much in common.

She always had a great affinity with the 'Paddies', too, and she loved to hear my stories of Ireland, the pure insanity that ran through the genes of our family, and the cosy tales of the homely fire and the wonderful characters who gathered around it.

Life changed dramatically for me and Colin after Dad sent us over the sea to Ireland, and I wondered if my Celtic roots had anything to do with how I'd ended up standing there in the witness box in the courtroom. I had mixed memories of my time in Ireland, some bad, some good. I remembered the constant humour and the way in which jokes could spread for miles until they'd completed a circle and ended up back at the start again, with extra funny bits added along the way.

For some reason, our family couldn't stay at my beloved Bramdene. Everything had to change. Dad booked the ferry, took us along to Holyhead and gave Agnes £20 to give to Moira to look after us. There was a to-do as we went on board the ferry, because Dad had paid for us to have a cabin but the porter said we didn't have one booked. Dad looked grief-stricken as he watched 16-year-old Agnes and me and Colin battle our way down to the third-class decks with all the drunks and tinkers. Colin and I didn't mind a bit, though, and I don't think Agnes did either, because as soon as she found a space for us on a bench, she went off to join the crowds, her big old beehive hairdo waving about as she tried to avoid the dirty old men with their lit fags. Colin had told her that hairspray was highly flammable, and he was quite an expert on the subject because he had once burned his eyebrows off while he was dismantling a banger. Agnes had called him a 'fecking little know-it-all' and pretended not to take a blind bit of notice, but we always used to peep in on her when she put her hairspray on to see what she was going to do with her fag. It always made us laugh.

Agnes had come over from Ireland supposedly to look after me and Colin while Dad was at work. Dad was having a complete nervous breakdown over what he could possibly do with two small kids and a full-time job while Mum did her disappearing act. But, like any 16 year old, Agnes had had other ideas, and she soon hooked up with Mum, who was not much older, and they would both disappear for days.

I don't think Agnes liked the thought of going back to Ireland, and she definitely didn't like the thought of taking us two with her. Colin and I sat on the bench in the lower decks, as we were told to, and enjoyed the dramas that unfolded around us. A call for the 'fella with the spoons' kicked off the entertainment, and pretty soon they all joined in, singing songs of their beloved homeland and hugging and promising to stay in touch with each other for ever, even though they never would.

When we arrived, Moira was far from delighted to see us. She had eighteen kids of her own, and the last thing she needed was two more mouths to feed. Colin and I tried to blend in with the others so that she wouldn't notice us. But when she got down or angry, we were her first targets – or at least I felt as though I was. Moira always used to call me a bold bitch, and I was always trying to duck out of her way when she was in a raging mood. I used to try to avoid her anyway, because I knew the 'sight of me' would set her off.

I didn't really mind staying at Moira's at first, because it was great having so many other kids around you constantly. Colin and I soon learned that we were but amateurs in learning to outwit the enemy. Colin fitted in with all the other kids straight away. He always seemed to know the right thing to say and how to get other people to agree with him without making them want to thump him. I still wanted to thump him, but apparently that was because, as he kept telling me, 'You don't listen.' Even Moira liked him, but they did have some massive fallings out. I kept falling out with everybody, and sometimes it felt as though I didn't have a friend in the world apart from my lovely granddad.

He spent all his days walking the length and breadth of the lanes in and around Lawrencetown. He was a retired blacksmith, Mum had told me, and for some reason he lived as a wandering tramp even though he owned most of the land around the village. My grandmother seemed to hate him, and he didn't have a bed or a bedroom; he just slept on the floor of the milk cupboard on rainy nights or when it was really cold, and she left old coats there for him. He didn't mind living rough – actually, he said he preferred it.

He could go where he wanted and do what he wanted, without anyone bossing him around. I knew what Granny was like, so I didn't blame him.

He was a real old 'smoky Joe', a king of the road in a huge, heavy overcoat with rope tied round the middle and mud-covered old boots that he never took off. He was a thin man, probably due to all that walking, and his face was covered in white hair. He wore a trilby that looked nearly as old as he was, and he smoked a pipe that he kept relighting and fiddling with. I was always glad when he stopped to fill his pipe, because then it meant we could have a sit down and a rest on one of the stone walls or lay-bys where you could always find him. Sometimes, if there were a few of us, we could persuade him to sing us a song and he would always do the voices and the actions and make us giggle.

He never wore a watch, but he always went back to the house at mealtimes when Granny would be dishing up food, and he used to take me, too, if I was with him. I liked going to Granny's house, because she was always cooking. They used to have the same thing every single day, but I never got bored of it. Granny had three bedrooms in her house: one for her, one for my Uncle Finbar* and one for Grady*. I was never really sure who Grady was and why he lived in the house; he used to work on the farm with Finbar, but he wasn't family. Some used to say my grandfather had taken him in when he was orphaned as a child and that the land owned by Grady's family joined ours. I never knew what was true, but I knew I didn't like him much. He growled a lot.

I loved my Uncle Finbar, though; he was always great fun. Granny was great fun, too, when she was in a good mood. She would teach me and Colin sad and soppy Irish folk songs, then pull in all the neighbours so she could get us to sing for them and make them cry. She said we had the voices of angels. We used to make her cry with laughter when she tried to teach us Irish dancing, because we never could get the hang of it, but we would do it for the neighbours, too, just for the craic of it.

Granny owned a huge farm – well, strictly speaking, I suppose my grandfather did, but that was a minor point. She was the matriarch of the entire town. Everyone called her 'Mammy' – even the shopkeepers and people from outside the town. Colin and I called her 'Granny' because we were English, but we soon did the same as all Moira's kids and called her Mammy, and we called Moira by her first name. Her kids never called her Mum.

It was always a special treat to go to visit Mammy, because she would always give you a cup of tea and a cut of bread with lashings of butter spread on so thick that you left your teeth prints behind. You could put as much sugar as you wanted into your tea, and you could even sprinkle some onto your bread and butter if no one was looking.

Mammy did all her cooking over a huge open fireplace. It had hooks of some sort hanging down from the middle bit, where Mammy would have a huge kettle constantly on the go, and at midday a huge pot of boiling bacon would be hung from another hook, then a tin bucket filled with potatoes fresh from the field with their skins and the muck still on them. Then Mammy would peel and chop up loads of turnips and throw them in with the bacon.

Mammy always made soda bread in the mornings. She would get up really early to start making it. I often used to watch her, because I was fascinated. She would leave bottles of milk high up on a shelf in the main room and then wait until the milk had curdled so much it had separated, before she could use it for the bread. She made the bread on a table next to a window where you could look out towards the road to Lawrencetown. Looking out from there, you always knew who was coming and going so you could talk about them before they arrived, and then again after they had left. I used to kneel up on the chair and lean onto the table with my elbows while she was making bread. She loved having someone to talk to – or, more accurately, someone to talk about – while she was pounding the dough in the big plastic washing-up bowl. I loved listening to the gossip, too, and passing it on, which got me a few belts round the head, but it didn't stop me. Mammy could be really nice to me when she was there on her own. It was only when the others were there that she used to show off and tease me for being posh and having an English accent.

When she made the bread, she would put the dough into a big, round iron pot, put the lid on it and then push it into the flames and pile red- and white-hot pieces of turf on top of it and all around. Everybody was always ready when the bread was taken out of the fire – I don't remember any clocks, so I suppose it was the smell that got them. Mammy had a unique way of handing out the bread once it had cooled down. She would sit in her armchair with the huge round of bread, using her left arm to strategically balance it on her enormous breasts while she brandished the breadknife with the other arm. She would cut off the crust like a skilled swordsman, then with a sharp flick of the bread knife scoop up a dollop of butter and slather it over the exposed slice before cutting it off and passing it to the nearest outstretched hand.

The fire was the heart of the home, constantly being topped up by huge bricks of blackened turf that would burn and go grey. I think Grady and Finbar used to go up to the bog to get it, and I may even have gone with them one time, as I remember them criss-crossing great big slabs of turf that they would cut into columns and then squares. Huge walls of these were stored in a barn next to the cowshed.

Mammy's farm was a huge, isolated bungalow with a main road running in front of it, dividing the fields. The main road was, of course, actually a narrow, winding country lane that saw a few tractors and one, maybe two cars a week. It was outside of Lawrencetown, where Moira lived, maybe two or even three miles away. If you went there after dark, you had to stay the night.

I had been lucky enough to sleep in Mammy's bed a couple of times, but it was always full, and Mammy always gave preference to Moira's kids over me, because I was way too high and mighty. When I had managed to squeeze in it was pure luxury! It had a soft sunken mattress and sheets and blankets and a huge fleece eiderdown with feathers that made me sneeze. I had felt like the Princess in 'The Princess and the Pea'! I didn't like it that much, though, because the other kids used to lie there, whispering and talking about me, saying horrible things. I would make out I was asleep, but I could hear everything they said and it made me sad.

I didn't care, though; I loved being with Granddad, and on cold nights he would help me climb up the back wall at Moira's so I could sneak in with the other kids, and then they would help me climb back out in the morning in case she caught me. I was happy to stay with Granddad, even though he didn't like the English because they had sent the Black and Tans into Lawrencetown and they had done terrible things. I used to tease him by saying I was English, but he would say 'no, you're not' or 'away with you' and wave his wobbly walking stick at me, but he couldn't catch me because he couldn't run. He didn't really mind my being English, though, because sometimes if we fell asleep in the barn looking up at the stars, I would wake up and find his coat over me. And he could always get us a cup of tea from somewhere. I hated having a cup of tea in Moira's because she didn't have enough cups and you had to wait until someone finished or else use a jam jar. Granddad knew all the best places!

Mammy's house only had one living area, with the huge fire to cook on and to keep the place warm, and a couple of armchairs. The three bedrooms came off the main room, and there was a large cupboard next to the front door. I remember the first time I stumbled on it, I was in awe. There were high wooden shelves all around the walls, and on the wooden shelves were huge silver bowls, but I couldn't see into them. However, I found that if I stood on my tiptoes, I could just about reach my hand over and dip my finger in. I had no idea what was in there, but I was willing to risk it. When there was no one around, I sneaked in there and reached up as high as I could and shakily lowered my hand. It was as if all my wishes had come true: it was pure cream and it was like nectar! From then on, I found the slightest excuse to go in there or did so when no one was looking. I even told Colin my big secret and made him swear, on pain of death, not to tell anyone else.

There was no bathroom and no toilet; you did your business at the back of the cowshed and you wiped your bum with a leaf. Baths were very few and far between because they involved so much effort. First you walked down to the pump, which I am sure was at least a mile away, and then you had to carry buckets and buckets of water back to the house to be heated up and poured into the tin bath in front of the fire. I was never allowed to carry a bucket back because I couldn't be trusted, so I used to just dance along to annoy the others.

The main washing water came from a huge black water tank at the back of the barn, which was filled with rainwater. It was why Mammy had such beautiful skin, she told us, because she washed her face with it every day. Sometimes she just used to egg on one of the others to tell her beautiful-skin story, so she could just sit there proudly and grin. I remember her scrubbing my face a couple of times with a slab of hard green soap, the same stuff she used to scrub the floor, and I tried not to let her catch me after that.

I also used to help her to collect the eggs and feed the chickens. There used to be chickens all over the place, just walking around the yard and field and laying eggs in the cowshed. Me and Mammy used to feed them with the peelings from the hot potatoes, and sometimes Mammy used to let me hold the bowl so that they would run after me while I threw the peelings on the ground. The chickens used to snooze and roost in the hay that the cows used to eat; they weren't bothered by the cows and the cows didn't seem to be bothered by them. They weren't bothered by me or Colin, either, because sometimes we used to sit up there for hours, waiting for one of them to lay an egg so that we could run in to Mammy with it.

Colin and I had to do a lot of hiding when we were in Ireland, in case anyone in authority started asking questions. We weren't going to school and no one was supposed to know we were there. I don't know why. This meant that we were hidden from the priest as well, so we never went to church with all the others. If a stranger came into the town, the word would spread in minutes and we were kept out of the way until they found out who it was. I had no idea how news could travel so fast; there were no telephones and few cars. I suspect it was very enthusiastic cousins who would turn up at Mammy's or Moira's on their bikes, all out of breath. 'Quick, quick,' they would say, 'there's a quare fella in Leitrim asking all sorts of questions.' You never really got to find out what sort of questions, because by the time you found out how Bridget Connell heard it from her cousin who is married to the man who works in Leitrim and spoke to a man at the station who was in the pub for a quick Guinness at lunchtime who heard the quare fella with his own ears it didn't really matter; it just meant that Colin and I had to vanish again and not open our big gobs to anyone and give ourselves away with our snobby English accents.

I had found a hidden stash of books in Mammy's amazing bedroom – stacks of Mills & Boon mini-novels that I read one after the other. I would steal a couple away and then find a quiet spot on a haystack, or in a field. When I searched Mammy's bedroom again, I came across some Agatha Christies. She wasn't angry when she found out it was me stealing her books; in fact, she found me a few more, and when the word went out people would turn up with all sorts of books for me. I read *Gulliver's Travels*, Edgar Allan Poe and my greatest joy, P.G. Wodehouse. Mammy loved it when relatives and neighbours dropped off their favourite books for me. 'Ah, well, we have always been big readers in our family,' she would tell them with her chin held up a few notches higher than usual, 'and Linda and Colin could read long before they went to school, you know.'

I loved all the books and read them avidly; they were my lifeline during the long, endless days when the others were at school and neither Moira nor Mammy had the patience for me. I especially liked the spooky stories, the short ones that made you jump at the end. I always used to try to hang around when the grown-ups were talking, especially at night, because they always told each other spooky stories, and if I could tell a story, too, they might like me and I might even get a meal and a bed. The stories would always scare the bejesus out of you, and, as far as I could tell, there were several banshees hanging around in the bushes all around Lawrencetown. If the storyteller had not seen the banshee personally, they had a friend, cousin or distant family member who was known for going to church every week and had never told a lie in their life and who had seen it. Their stories always seemed to get bolder as they drank more Guinness. I would lie on the floor, hoping no one would notice I was still there, and listen in awe. Then I would repeat the stories to the other kids, adding bits to make them even scarier.

To me, the Irish seemed to talk a lot more than the English, and often they would introduce the most obscure subject and no one would bat an eyelid. But most of the time a story would start off with an old story like, 'Do you remember that time Finbar lost those two rams?', and all the grown-ups would look down towards the ground, shaking their heads as they tried to recall their own personal memory of that fateful night. Then they would all take turns, remembering where they were and what they were doing, and those stories would lead off into other stories. Most of the stories were about death, such as who had just died even though they looked marvellous only the day before, and then talk about who was hanging on by a 'tred'. Then they would all make the sign of the cross simultaneously and say 'God rest her soul' or 'bless her' if they were talking about the still very much alive old trollop who lived up the road. No one could even remember the last time they had seen her in church, 'the aul whoor, bless her'. Then Moira or one of them would shake a fist at me and say, 'And if ya repeat any of that, ya bold bitch, you'll get the hiding of yer life.' Unfortunately, some of the stories were way too juicy to keep to myself, so in the end they would kick me out before they got to the best bits so I couldn't hear them. I found, however, that if I buried my head in a book they wouldn't notice me and I could make out I wasn't listening, even if I was.

And then the stories would take on a life of their own and spread from town to county. Someone could drive through from County Clare a couple of months later and ask, 'Did Finbar ever find those two rams?'

No one believed my stories after the banshee incident, but it wasn't really my fault. I had cadged a lift on the back of my cousin

Eileen's* pushbike going up to Mammy's one night, and I thought I saw a light. 'I thought I saw a light,' I said to Eileen casually as she huffed and puffed, pushing down onto the pedals and cursing me for the extra weight. I only said it because I thought I should speak to her to cheer her up. She was the one doing all the hard work. She was so angry at what I had said that she let go of the handlebars so she could turn around and whack me. 'Ye little bitch,' she was yelling as the bike veered off the road and we both ended up in the ditch. I nearly killed Eileen with the fright of it, because I didn't know that that particular bend in the lane was well known for banshees lurking in the bushes and flashing lights.

When Eileen finally stopped whacking me round the head she started shaking me and telling me to tell her what I had seen. I think it had just been the reflection of the bike's headlamp, but if I told her that she would fecking kill me. 'I don't know what I saw,' I said as I helped her pull the bike out of the ditch, 'but I definitely saw something.' We walked back, with her pushing her bike, calling on Jesus, Mary and Joseph and telling me she hoped Mammy would fecking batter me if I was lying. 'Didn't you see the bushes rustling?' I asked.

She stopped pushing the bike and stood there thinking for a moment. Then she said, 'You know, I think I might have done,' and went back to calling on Jesus, Mary and Joseph.

By the time we arrived at Mammy's, we were both screeching we had seen a ghost. We were quickly doused in holy water and told to stand there and say three Hail Marys before we were allowed to tell the story.

Mammy told Grady to 'feck off out of his armchair' and let me sit there, and one of them handed me and Eileen a cup of tea while my cousin Kathleen* ran up the road to get Mary Kelly, because she would know what to do.

'Was it a banshee?' Mammy asked me gently. I didn't have a clue, but they were all gathering around for a story, so, eyeing up the bread on the table, I decided to follow my instincts.

'It might have been,' I said as timidly as I was able to, and I remembered to make my hands tremble so I would look like I had just had the fright of my life.

'Did it howl?' asked Agnes, and she bent forwards, looking at me suspiciously with her arms folded tightly in front of her. I could see by the puss on her that she didn't believe a word I was saying. 'Because that one Bridget Connell saw up there definitely howled.' She stood upright, leaned backwards, tilted her chin and stared around the room with a smug gob on her, as if to say, 'Got you, you little bitch.'

I looked towards Mammy, who had her hands squeezed so tightly in prayer I could see her white knuckles and she was looking down at me with bated breath, waiting to hear my next words. 'Yes, I am almost certain I heard it howl,' I confirmed, nodding my head angelically and looking over to Eileen with big cow eyes, pleading with her to back me up.

'Yeah, I think I heard a howl, too,' Eileen said, not very convincingly, I thought. And you could tell she didn't say it to help me; she said it because she was getting pampered, too. 'But I couldn't be sure,' she added and glared at me with eyes that said, 'I'll fecking kill you later.'

Agnes was still standing next to Mammy with her arms folded, and from the look on her face I wasn't sure which one of them would get me first. 'Jesus, Mary and Joseph,' Mammy shrieked at Agnes, 'would you leave the poor child alone.' And then she glared around the room and said, 'And don't anyone say another word until Mary Kelly gets here.' Then she blessed herself again with the holy water.

Mary Kelly had seen the banshee long before Bridget Connell, so she was a bit of an authority on the whole area of banshees. They all moved to make way for her as she arrived, and she headed straight towards me and bent down to peer into my face, looking for signs, while someone shoved a chair behind her. As I watched Mary sit down, I could hear Agnes saying, 'Don't listen to her, Mary, she's a known liar,' but Mammy gave her a slap around the head and told her to shut the feck up. 'And she's a bold bitch,' Agnes mumbled under her breath. I knew she would wallop me later, but I thought I might as well hang for a sheep as for a lamb, and I took another bite out of the cut of bread I had in my hands.

They interrogated me for ages, and I kept adding bits on because I was enjoying all the attention. The rustle I had heard turned into something with a definite shape, and the shape became a woman. I was sure of that. Then someone suggested calling out the priest, but they couldn't because then 'they' would know I was there and there would be hell to pay. Everyone eventually went off to bed wondering what was to be done, and I climbed into Mammy's bed because I was allowed to sleep in the middle next to her.

When I told the woman who ran the grocery shop that I was the child who had seen the banshee, she invited me in and sat me on the counter so I could tell her the whole story. After I told it to her the first time she gave me a few broken biscuits, and if she saw me hanging about she would call me in to tell her customers.

'It was definitely a woman,' I would say, 'all dressed in white, like she was wearing a shroud.' This usually drew a few sharp intakes of breath and a few Jesus, Mary and Josephs, so I would pause for that bit and then carry on with my story.

'And did she have long hair?' someone would usually ask.

'Yep, right down past her waist, and jet black,' I said, and I would bend my arm behind my back to show them how far down her hair came. I picked up quite a few things about banshees in the following few days because it was the talk of the village, so I was always able to add a few bits on. I think I was starting to lose credibility in the end, and eventually the grocery shop lady got a bit fed up hearing it over and over. Not keen to give up all those biscuits, sweets and coins so easily, I used to wait outside until someone who hadn't heard it 'straight from the child's mouth' walked up to the shop.

After a few days, everyone got fed up with my story and I was running out of people to tell it to. 'Did you go and tell the Clancys?' Mammy would ask me when I was getting on her nerves. And when she was really fed up with me, she would think of a neighbour who lived miles away who hadn't heard the story and who always had cake in the house.

I think I went too far, eventually, because I kept hearing the words 'bold bitch' when people were talking about me, and then some of them would say quite openly, even to Mammy's face, that a priest should be called and there might have to be an exorcism. I had read a short story about the Salem witches and I knew what things like that could lead to. I spent many strange hours lying under haystacks pondering on whether I would prefer to be hanged or burned at the stake. The guilt and torment of it all was killing me, because I couldn't decide which would be quickest and less painful, the burning or the hanging.

In the end, I had to confess that I hadn't really seen a banshee; I probably hadn't even seen a light. I wasn't sure about the howl, because that might have been a fox or even Eileen screaming her big gob off. I looked accusingly at Eileen, because it was all her fault anyway. She was determined to shift the blame back on me so she reminded everyone that she had said that she 'couldn't be sure' at the time. They all stared at me. I knew there wasn't any point in saying, 'I couldn't help it, it wasn't my fault,' because I had committed the worst sin ever heard of, and all the penance in the world wouldn't take that away. I was shamed, a complete outcast. I had been reading lots of Mills & Boon, so I knew what it was like to be cast out of society.

At that moment I hated them. All of them. And I could see that they all hated me, but I wasn't going to cry, because all my favourite Mills & Boon heroines would hold on to their pride and fight to hold back their tears. I grabbed my books off the kitchen table and ran out of the door, determined never to return to any of their houses ever again. I decided I was never, ever going to speak again and that I was going to live in the fields for ever and drink water from the spring. I wasn't bothered about food, I wanted them to find my poor wasted body and feel guilty for not feeding me. I felt better when I pictured their fake sad faces when they would have to lie to the priest about what happened to me.

I ran off across the field, and then into another, and another, but made sure to keep my eye on the stream so I could find my way back. All the time I was wondering whether it might be more dramatic if I died of consumption. Heroines who died of consumption were very highly thought of, and it might teach that lot more of a lesson than if I were to starve.

I wanted to find my granddad to tell him about my plan, and I walked for miles, but I eventually gave up and lay down under a haystack to have a read and a snooze. I chose a haystack in sight of the house, because I knew they wouldn't bother looking for me, and I didn't know how long I could last out with the hunger pangs.

I lay back on the straw and held my book up to shield myself from the burning sun, happy in the knowledge that the guilt they would all feel over my sudden demise would kill them. At that moment I really missed my mum and dad, and I wondered when I would ever see them again.

I had no idea how long Colin and I had been out in Ireland – days, weeks and months had just run into each other – until one day my father and mother both turned up together. They had sent a telegram to say they were coming, and Mammy had to send someone out to find us. My cousin Rose* found me out helping Finbar feed turnips to the cows and she dragged me back to Mammy's, promising me either a great surprise or a clip around the head, she couldn't quite make up her mind which. Rose was a few years older than me, but I wasn't scared of her. She liked teasing me for having airs and graces, but she could be a good laugh sometimes.

When we got to Mammy's, she already had the tin bath out in front of the kitchen fire. Strictly speaking, the kitchen was the living room, too, and it was the only place in which to have a bath. It was very public, but nobody ever took a blind bit of notice of anyone in the bath in the nip, life just carried on around them. I avoided them at all costs, because you always ended up bloody freezing. Happily, no one ever chased me about this because a bath was such a palaver to organise.

Colin was standing there shivering with a towel wrapped round him, and I could see from the scummy water that I definitely wasn't going to be the first to have used the bath. Mammy and Rose were trying to hurry me up and get me in the water while it was still warm, and Mammy shouted out, 'Would somebody dry that poor gossoon before he catches his death,' adding a quick 'Jesus, Mary and Joseph' onto the end of it. When Mammy and Rose took a look at my hair to decide whether to scrub it with carbolic soap or washing-up liquid, they both shrieked and looked away. I couldn't remember the last time anybody had brushed or combed it, and it grew upwards and outwards so that I looked like a mini madwoman in the attic. I heard one of them say, 'We'll never get a brush through it again,' and then they went back to their whispering as Rose toyed with the scissors. I didn't care; I was splashing about in the water and lowering myself down as far as my shoulders. Colin was dancing up and down now, saying, 'Mum and Dad are coming, Mum and Dad are coming.' I didn't know whether to believe him, but no one was going to get their hands on my hair! I wondered if I could make a run for it.

'Sure, doesn't Squeezy give it a nice shine?' I heard Mammy say as she walked towards me with Rose hot on her heels. Before I knew it, Rose had got me in a headlock and Mammy was telling her to lower me gently so she could pour the water. I could see the look of glee on Rose's face. I didn't trust her one bit! I waited until she had lowered her head down near my gob, then I screamed as loud as I could. I have no idea why I did that, because, naturally, she immediately let go of me and my head went under the water. I decided to carry on screaming and being a brat, because they would have to be nice to me: Mum and Dad were coming! Naturally, I had decided to milk it for all it was worth.

The day was frantic; people were running errands here, there and everywhere. 'Go and ask Mrs Reilly if she's still got that nice milk jug and can I borrow it,' I heard Mammy say as she shoved my cousin Veronica* out the door, 'and ask Bridey if I can have a loan of her china plates.' Everyone was cleaning up and putting on their

Sunday clothes. Mammy even put her teeth in and a bit of lipstick on. Colin and I had to sit and not 'touch anything, do anything, or go anywhere'. No, we couldn't go and see if the chickens had laid any eggs. No, we couldn't go and help Grady milk the cows. We were to sit there and keep our traps shut. It felt as though we were all sitting there waiting for hours, and we probably were. It was a long aul journey from London, and we had no phones and no way of knowing when somebody would arrive.

I remember the moment, of course. It was Dad and Mum, and they looked so smart and so happy, Dad in his suit, Mum in her miniskirt and with her beehive hair. I don't know who I ran to first, but I was crying and laughing, I had missed them so much. Colin held back, and as they walked through the door he ran and hid behind a chair and wouldn't come out. It took them ages to persuade him, but when he did he ran to Dad and hugged him, and then he threw his arms around Mum and cried into her shoulder. We were together again, but it wouldn't be for long. In fact, soon Ireland was to become another blurry, hazy memory of the girl I used to be.

Chapter 27

The Sledgehammer and the Rock

My memories of Ireland drifted away. I was stronger than Omni thought I was. I remembered so well the child I used to be, and she wouldn't have been afraid, she would have spoken up.

I once read about a woman who had a recurring dream. She could see a little girl in the distance, but she could never catch her. But one day she finally did, and she picked her up, and she hugged her, and she loved her, and then she realised that the little girl was her, the way she used to be before life's cruel blows had changed her beyond recognition.

That story meant a lot to me, and I remembered that little girl that I used to be with the crazy haircuts and the laughter always bubbling beneath the surface, and it gave me strength.

I remembered how the defendants' psychologist had squirmed in the witness box – at least that was what it looked like to me, as though he still had a conscience and wanted to be anywhere else but there. He looked like one of those professors who have read and written so many books that they have forgotten what life is like in the real world. I imagined he would have much preferred to have been sitting in his library, leaning back in his big comfy armchair and trying to find the answer to the bigger picture. I sort of pictured him smoking a pipe, too; it would go with the haircut he had forgotten to have and his casual, careless but still smart outfit that said, 'I just threw this on because I have much better things to think about than the rest of you.' He kept repeating, 'This is one of the most shocking childhoods I have ever seen.' But he kept his head turned towards the papers in front of him, and he sounded sad as he said it. He wouldn't look up at me; in fact, he wouldn't look up at anyone.

The cold, imposing atmosphere of the courtroom had worn me down. I felt as though someone had crawled inside my head and was sifting through it, digging out my worst nightmares, my night terrors, those horrible thoughts from the past that I could usually swish away with my Scarlett O'Hara line: 'I'll think about that tomorrow.' Omni and the icy cold formality of the courtroom had reduced me to another number, another case from that day's list, another penniless, soulless, gibbering claimant. Of course, they would all have to listen to the entire case carefully, and they all made their own notes for posterity, ever ready to pick up on any deviation from a script or a flaw in a witness's evidence, hastily passing secret notes back and forth across the benches and silently nodding to acknowledge their contents.

The witness box put me higher than the rows of benches, and even higher than Omni, but he had a way of looking down his nose at me that made me feel as though I was standing in front of him like a naughty child, small and insignificant, one of the lower orders that he was graciously giving his precious time to.

He had thrown out his killer accusations – 'your mother rejected you' and 'you were found in a hovel' – and then he had stood back to enjoy each victory and to savour each wound to the heart. Like a gladiator, he looked around to his audience and to the judge, his emperor, waiting for the thumbs up or thumbs down, the go-in-for-the-kill signal. The judge looked down on Omni with an almost tender, fatherly indulgence as he swirled his cloak and raised and lowered his affected voice, like a hammy Laurence Olivier, basking in the affection of the crowd.

He was a wordsmith, but so was I, and I hadn't lost a battle of words for as long as I could remember. I knew that I wasn't like other claimants, I knew that I would rise to the occasion, that I wouldn't crumble in the witness box. I loved centre stage, I loved the sound of my own voice, and I was more than capable of being a drama queen, too.

I had spent my entire life reading and researching, desperate to know, to understand the strange, formidable place that was St Anne's Convent. I needed to know how, why and where the cruelty I had encountered there had come from.

I had discovered so much in the years leading up to the trial, so many tragedies among my peers, former boarders of St Anne's. I was struck by how our lives had run parallel: we suffered the same emotional problems, the same relationship traumas, the same financial hardship and the same alienation from our siblings.

And I had learned about childhood invulnerables when I studied the life of one of my heroes, Charlie Chaplin, and I wanted and needed to be one. A childhood invulnerable is a psychological term for a child who suffers unimaginable trauma yet remains resilient, street smart and successful, almost dedicating their lives to putting right the wrongs that they have experienced growing up.

In a strange way, my whole court case had become a kind of crusade. I learned that a cash award, even on the present scales, could, in so many cases, be the lifeline that the claimant desperately needed. I had survived my experiences, although I had my eccentricities, but I was coherent and I was still standing. And I was determined to give Omni a run for his money.

As I finished giving my evidence, I thought of Philip, a wonderful boy with great expectations who had been found dead in a grotty council flat, cause of death unknown. And who cared? I thought of Philip as I faced my adversary, and I thought of all the Philips out there.

I had stood in the witness box, the tears pouring down my face unashamedly. 'He killed Philip,' I had told them, 'and he is killing Karen and Hugh, too, because they are not long for this world . . . unless they get help.'

'Peter Rands did not kill Philip,' Omni replied. 'Philip died, on his own, in a flat . . .'

I interrupted him. I wouldn't let him finish. I was too angry. 'Yes, he did kill Philip, just as surely as if he had stuck a dagger into his heart.'

'You have no evidence . . .'

Omni was droning on. But I wouldn't let him speak. I wasn't speaking for myself now; I was speaking for all the others, the ones who would never get a chance to speak out and to tell their stories.

It seemed to me that the whole courtroom was crying, and the judge said, 'I think we will take a break here,' but as I turned to get out of the witness box, he reminded me that I was still under oath before he gestured that it was OK for me to step down. As I walked back down the aisle towards the back seats, I felt as though all eyes were on me and people were wondering if I was a lunatic. Some were wiping away tears.

Big Lynn had been standing at the back of the court with her arms outstretched to hug me, her eyes red with crying. I had wanted to speak to my lawyer, my barrister, my psychologist, but all of them put their fingers to their lips, and said, 'Shh, not allowed to talk about the case.' I was under oath and not allowed to speak about the case to anyone connected with it, nor were they allowed to speak to me about it. I was desperate to know how I was doing. Was it OK? What did they think? And Lynn even made thumbs-up hand gestures to them to try to get them to nod one way or the other. They could speak to me, it seemed, but they couldn't talk about the case.

During the recess, everyone wandered off in different directions, and Lynn and I strolled the unfamiliar Leeds streets looking for a sandwich bar. Two war-weary, menopausal, middle-aged women, sweating profusely from our hormones and stress, we were both traumatised and could only manage to speak in disjointed, short, sharp sentences. No explanations were necessary; we had been friends for nearly 40 years and knew each other's moods and how to react to them.

We had plonked ourselves wearily on the steps of a museum, chain-smoking and sipping steaming coffee out of polystyrene cups, which we used to warm our hands. The weather had turned chilly. Big Lynn soon perked up as she tucked into yet another wonderful sandwich from the local baker's. Lynn always opened a sandwich as if it were her first present on Christmas Day, with such joy and excitement that it was impossible to stay sombre in her presence. Her incessant upbeat chatter couldn't fail to bring me back to reality.

My life hadn't been a disaster; I had changed it midway through. I had hit a watershed, I had taken the road less travelled and I had found contentment, of sorts. But more than anything, I had found the courage to face up to my former tormenters and to speak out for the others whom I had failed so long ago.

Chapter 28

My Epiphany

The vow I had made to myself as a child just wouldn't go away. I have called myself a 'writer' since the age of 13 – yes, I was indeed that snooty. I had stored up my memories for a reason, but I never really knew what that reason was – or else I simply hadn't wanted to tackle them. I wanted to write about anything other than the convent, though I knew in my heart that one day I would have to.

I had little contact with my mother after we left the convent. Dad had qualified as a psychiatric nurse and got a council house and taken us home. Mum was still moving around all the time, never settling anywhere for long. The few times I did see her, she always seemed to bring chaos and lunacy into my life. It was no wonder I was a neurotic heap. On top of that, I was constantly reading all Dad's psychology textbooks and had stupidly decided it was 'the mother to blame'. To my shame, I cut her out of my life. I had had enough grief already.

In defence of my mum and dad, they were good people, and they loved Colin and me to pieces. They drank too much, they fought, they made terrible decisions, but their love for us was never in doubt. As immigrants to this country, they faced prejudice, unemployment, homelessness and poverty.

Unfortunately, my brother Colin was an angry young man. Angry with Mum, angry with Dad and angry with me. He could not and would not talk about the convent or anything that happened there. I do not blame him for that one bit. At the age of 17, Colin went off to see the world – quite literally. He packed his bag, took off and the next we heard from him, he was in the Highlands of Scotland waiting to join up with a fishing boat. From there, he went on the oil rigs and he called us from places like Norway and Dallas, Texas, and once even from a street market in the Punjab. Dad and I treasured his phone calls, his visits home and tales of his exploits. He has grown up to be a strong, confident man, successful in his career and with a wonderful family. I am endlessly proud of him.

By the time I was 21, I was married and had a beautiful baby boy, and by the time I was 22 I wanted to kill my husband. I hung on in there until we reached the statutory period of three years after which I could get a divorce.

My next major relationship led to another beautiful baby boy, and his father and I spent the next fifteen years knocking seven bells out of each other before I realised I had to change my life for good. I had always worked, though my home life was often disastrous, and I had always kept my two sons with me, protecting them as best I could, even if that meant protecting them from my mother.

I raised my boys alone, with the constant support of my beloved father, and as I grew closer to my mother, I had her support too. I worked constantly. At times I juggled two jobs to keep our heads above water. I was never really afraid of poverty, or even abandonment; I had experienced them and they hadn't killed me. My blasé attitude often made me reckless, and too often I had allowed my life and those of my sons to descend into chaos. Writing or burying my head in a book, I much preferred being 'away with the fairies' to coping with the reality of paying bills or doing chores. I always worked, but I always grew bored, and I would turn up late or use my sledgehammer wit in the workplace at an inopportune point, thus ensuring a 'Can you leave now?' moment and an escort to the door.

Then I finally had my epiphany! That moment I had been waiting for all my life, that sign from above, that blinding light, that call to grace. But it wasn't quite like that, of course. It came about after a chance meeting with an older and much wiser woman, and my coming across a hill full of foxes.

In my endless quest to keep a roof over my and my sons' heads, I had taken a job selling double glazing. It was a soulless, thankless job in which there was no satisfaction whatsoever to be found, and to add insult to injury you had to use your own petrol to chase leads as far as 60 miles away! As I drove around in the dark knocking on doors and disturbing people's cosy nights indoors, I used to try to make myself feel less guilty by telling myself, 'Well, they're better off than me, and at least they aren't out at all hours of the night selling windows.'

One day, as I walked towards some sheltered-housing scheme flats with my demonstration window under one arm and briefcase under the other, I felt absolutely awful. The thought of trying to persuade a vulnerable old lady to buy my overpriced windows sickened me, but I knew that if I didn't do it one of the other bastards I worked with would, and I hadn't had a call all day or a sale for more than a week.

The lady I had arranged to meet greeted me warmly and offered me a cup of tea straight away. I remember that I was overawed by the immediate warmth of the flat, not in the sense of coming in out of the cold; rather, it was a feeling that I find difficult to describe. Her walls were covered in a mad array of pictures and paintings, and she was filling up with joy as she told me the history behind each one I pointed out. I was a captive audience and was loving her stories, but I knew that if I didn't run through my spiel my boss would kill me. Phone calls from the boss during the sale were part of the routine, so there was no way of avoiding it.

I started part one of my well-rehearsed speech when she laughed and said, 'Oh, do come and sit down, I'm going to buy your silly windows.' I laughed as well, because at that moment I could see how insignificant those windows were.

Cynthia, I quickly found out, was a retired professor of history and she was South African. Her voice was mesmerising, her strong South African accent clipped and almost brusque, I thought, when compared with, say, the soft, flowing lilt of an Irish accent. I have always been fascinated by other nationalities and others' history and culture, and Cynthia's life story was as amazing as Churchill's. She had lived and worked through apartheid and she had fought for the cause. She had deep, insightful knowledge on every subject we discussed, and she became animated and excited as she realised how much I was enjoying her mini lectures. She had loved teaching, she told me, and from her collection of gifts of ornaments and *objets d'art*, it was obvious that her former students had loved her.

Her living room was small but truly cosy with a huge sofa and two large, comfortable armchairs around a fire and a small TV in the corner. 'Oh, I rarely put it on,' she told me. She was hugely proud of her vast collection of books, which filled the shelves that lined the entire back wall of her living room from floor to ceiling. She was more than happy for me to browse through the shelves, squealing with delight as I found books I had read and curious to know all about the ones that I was looking forward to. I teased her about her little footstool and warned her about the dangers of falling off it, but she just said, 'Yes, dear,' and didn't take a blind bit of notice.

She said she kept every book she had ever had, and the ones she loved the most she kept on the lower shelves. She had been married for more than 50 years but was recently divorced and had always promised herself wall-to-wall books when she had a place of her own. She had promised herself lots of things. Not for her queuing in supermarkets or watching the pennies. She ate the finest food, courtesy of a gourmet delivery service, and she even had a collection of the finest wines and sherries. But I guessed that books were her greatest love. Her collection wasn't in any order, and the dearest ones were well thumbed and easy to reach.

We spoke for hours – or, more importantly, I listened to Cynthia speak. It seemed as though she had found the secret to inner happiness, a kind of contentment that was so alien to me and one that I never dreamed could be possible for myself. I didn't feel stupid telling her that I wanted to be writer. 'Why not?' she said, and I didn't really have an answer for that. Well, I did, I had hundreds, but nothing real, nothing tangible. I told her I wanted to be a history teacher, too, that it had always been my dream but also that it wasn't an achievable one. I had two kids to raise; I struggled with jobs from one week to the next. It was impossible, wasn't it? Besides which, people like me didn't get degrees. It was daft, unheard of.

I left her home at about two o'clock, or it might even have been three in the morning. It was still dark as I drove through the winding country lanes, and my head was buzzing with what-ifs, perhapses and maybes. Cynthia had made it seem that my dreams were possible; they were not pie in the sky. I had no A levels, and I had never finished that psychology course I had started all those years ago. Could it be true? Was there really such a thing as a second chance? Although it was dark, the moon seemed to be shining brightly, and as I looked over at the fields I saw a scene that quite literally took my breath away. I stopped the car and gazed in wonder at the drama playing out before my eyes. There was a hill filled with foxes, and they were all looking in the same direction, towards the top. At the top of the hill stood a lone fox, an alpha male, his head tilted backwards as he howled at the moon.

I spent the next couple of years trying to put it to the back of my mind. The real world was difficult enough to cope with. I had gone back to my former job as a legal secretary, hating every minute of it, but it paid more than any of the other jobs I had tried, and I had found a solicitor's that would let me type during the night, so I could have two jobs.

My body gave out before my head. I was working in an eighth-floor office in the centre of Covent Garden, and as I leaned out of the window having a fag, looking down at all the regular people having fun, I felt huge griping pains in my stomach and then in my chest. I was alone in the building and doubled up in agony from pain so severe that it took my breath away. How I got through that night shift I will never know; I was so close to calling an ambulance.

I knew that I had to see my GP urgently and even take a day off to do so. I felt so ill that I had no option. At the same time, I felt ridiculous going in to see my GP, because the pains were coming and going – they weren't constant. I intended to make it a quick appointment and I didn't want to make a fuss, but before I could stop myself I blurted out that I thought I had ravaging consumption. I had expected the doctor to dismiss my fears with a prescription and a sick note, but, strangely, he took me seriously, and he sent me for every test imaginable, even sending a psychiatrist to my home. I always wonder what people mean when they talk about a nervous breakdown, but even as a sceptic I have to acknowledge that that probably was what I had.

I blubbed as I spoke to the psychiatrist, and I told him that all the problems I had probably stemmed back to my mother. I had read a lot of self-help books, and it was usually the mother who got the blame. He wanted to admit me to hospital immediately, but it was impossible; I had two sons to look after. He eventually got me to agree to a weekly visit to a cognitive therapist at the local psychiatric hospital. It took up the best part of a whole day, but as I went along each week I began to feel better. I began to accept that there was little or nothing that I could do about my financial troubles other than go along to the local Citizens Advice Bureau and sort out a budget. I was advised to go along and claim benefits. I was ill, and I needed to rest, and I had to accept it.

The weekly therapy sessions became a lifeline, and I learned to accept that I was not weird, that people didn't look at me funny or avoid me in social situations. I learned that I had a heightened sense of justice and injustice, and that was probably why I got the sack so often. If I didn't act in the same way as other people, what did it matter? Who were they to judge? I was actually a nice person, and I needed to like myself, and I needed to accept myself.

As my confidence grew, I began to go to the library, go for walks in the park and I even took up a week's free trial at my local gym. I also began to look for courses at the local library. It was summertime, and I had stumbled on courses that were due to begin within weeks.

I had looked at courses on and off for years, but usually I would just spend hours poring over them, daydreaming about what could be. Then real life would step in, and the college supplements and brochures would sink to the bottom of the pile and fade away.

This time, however, it was different. One course, an HND in professional writing, caught my eye, and I decided to call the number. Almost immediately I got through to Neil Nixon, the lecturer who had put the course together, and he told me to come along there and then for a chat. We spoke for ages, and he even sat outside with me so that I could have a cigarette!

As I walked away, I realised that I had signed away the next three years of my life, and at the grand old age of 41 I was to become a full-time student. The words of my dad and of Cynthia were echoing in my ears: there really was nothing to stop me. I knew that I would lose my house, our home, but it was beyond my control. And accepting that it was beyond my control was the biggest breakthrough.

When I returned to my therapist, I was so excited to tell her what I had done, but our session began to take on a different tone. She was telling me that this was our last time, and that I didn't need to come any more. It felt like a huge blow, but she gently explained that I was better, that I was OK, that I simply didn't need it, that was all. Then she looked at me curiously and said, 'You have no idea how ill you were when you first came here.' For a moment I felt devastated, deserted even, but I could understand what she was saying.

I didn't feel the same as the other outpatients who attended the centre; they had gone further down the depression route than I could ever imagine. I wasn't like them, and I didn't want to be. Somehow the therapy, or the bloody great big watershed I had crashed into, had had a huge impact on my life. I felt as though the part of me that had been lost so many years ago was starting to come back.

I didn't even feel ridiculous becoming a full-time student at such a grand old age. My father had gone into psychiatric nursing at the same age, and it was one of many things he had done that had made me so proud of him. Besides which, Neil had assured me that I wasn't going to be the oldest on my course. There were a couple of women who were a similar age to myself, and even one in her 60s.

As I enrolled on the course, I felt as though a new door had opened, a new life had started, and that things would never be the same again.

Day Three

Chapter 29

The Last Day: Floodgates

The final day of the trial was a blur. The learned barristers for both the claimant and the defendants took centre stage to perform their closing arguments. When they weren't quoting cases, which was just boring, their arguments were quite brilliant. But after listening to Omni, even I would have sent me home with a flea in my ear. I had had ample opportunity to come forward sooner, but, like most former boarders, the ability to blank it all out had served me well over the years.

I had been trying to discern whether there was any point-scoring going on, but it was difficult to tell: all the faces in the courtroom were expressionless, devoid of any humanity whatsoever. Like rejects from *Thunderbirds*, they looked as though they had had the life sucked out of them so only shells remained.

The judge had smiled at me a couple of times while I was in the witness box, but his smiles had been contrived: they were part of his role. I knew the smiles were meant for me because he was looking in my direction, and I stood alone, but there was no eye contact. I imagined it must have been hard for the judge to remain impartial, and I didn't envy him his job. Whatever judgment he passed would be added on to, or even buried in, the mountains of case law and precedents that had gone before, waiting for some eagle-eyed law student to spot its merits for use in another case. I quite liked the idea of being used as a precedent – I just hoped that it would be a good one.

I knew that my case was different in some way, and I wondered why it had come so far. In many ways, it was weak in comparison to others, and I vainly thought I had been chosen because I was articulate and I was strong. But I sensed it went much further.

Omni was still in full flow, but I clearly heard the word 'floodgates', and I had one of those 'hallelujah' moments, a moment where my suspicions seemed to be confirmed. If I were to win my case, it could open the door to potentially hundreds of others from the same care home and indeed from other Catholic children's homes in England.

The Church had come face to face with the results of their 'sweep it under the carpet' policies many times and were struggling to keep out of cases like mine. Economically they are probably thinking, 'Only about 20 years to go and they will all be dead by then, and if not they will lose on the limitation point.'

I knew that the Irish government and the Catholic Church had admitted liability in Ireland and that claimants no longer had to go through the ordeal of litigation and going to trial. The Church had accepted that abuse had occurred in the homes run by the Sisters of Mercy, and it is enough now for claimants simply to prove that they were in those institutions.

In England, the Catholic Church has denied liability, therefore every claimant must prepare for trial and prove their case. In the summer of 2010, both Rita and I did interviews for ITV, and following the broadcast there was a global apology from the Church for abuse – abuse that they denied in court. That lot sure must keep God busy with all their 'bless me, Father, because I have sinned' pleas.

I could see what Omni meant by 'floodgates', and I am pretty sure I saw the judge raise an eyebrow fractionally. My case was different, but it had nothing to do with my good speaking voice: I was only a pawn.

For me, Omni had made it so personal when he had attacked my family. I had spent so many years alienated from my mother because I had begun to blame her for everything, and I wondered how many other families had been torn apart.

I did indeed feel as if my case could be the tip of the iceberg. I sat there daydreaming about poking nests of hornets and awakening sleeping tigers. I thought that if I were in America they would make one of those TV movies about me. I wondered if they could get Sally Field for the part. According to my son, I looked exactly like her when she had played the role of Sybil, a woman with multiple personalities. I am not sure if I should have been flattered by that. I just thought she was brilliant at playing the unhinged.

Omni had made lots of good points. His star witness was, of course, the ghostly presence of Miss Bradshaw, that little old lady in her tweed suit with her crocheted beret and her brogues, the dedicated social worker who had kept meticulous notes of every visit, phone call or correspondence she had with me and Colin. Her evidence had been the defendants' ace card, and I couldn't really blame Omni for using it.

I didn't blame Miss Bradshaw one bit; her notes were accurate. Colin and I hadn't told her what was going on. She had asked us the right questions and we had given her the right answers. She hadn't really delved any further, but people didn't in those days. I had even smiled at the barely hidden irritation in her later notes, as she tried to put a positive spin on the fact that I was away with the fairies. It seemed I had discovered boys and didn't want to talk about anything else. It looked as though she had signed me off, almost angrily: 'Linda will do well, whatever she chooses to do.'

Miss Bradshaw wasn't the pantomime baddie of this drama; she was a social worker of her time, and Colin and I had adored her. She was a highly efficient one, too, if the reams and reams of documents were anything to go by.

I thanked the dear departed Miss Bradshaw profusely in my head. It felt as though the spirit of that conscientious, pen-pushing old lady was hovering over the courtroom. The most important thing for me was that she had delivered us to the convent in 1968 as happy, bright, well-adjusted children. After that, she had made a note of my silence and the change in my character in her records. She had even questioned me as to why I'd changed, but I could never have told her then.

I had trusted Miss Bradshaw implicitly, and even as the trial came to an end my opinion of her hadn't changed. I believed that she had been right when she described me as a 'happy child', and it had sent me off on a journey of discovery in my head. I had believed her over all the expert reports, the years of therapy, the self-help books, the navel-gazing and the Scarlett O'Hara impressions. Maybe her evidence proved my case, not theirs?

As impressed as I was with Omni's performance, his voice had gone off into that ecumenical drone of the pompous and my mind had started to wander. I thought about how I had cried like a baby in the witness box a day earlier, and I cringed at the thought. I had looked like shit because I had overslept and I hadn't had a shower, and my hastily applied mascara had gone vertical so that I had looked like a deranged drag queen. 'You don't look as glamorous as you did yesterday,' my young, fresh and immaculate barrister had pointed out to me as we stood outside the court building, having a quick fag. She was in great spirits: she looked as though she had swum ten lengths before breakfast, undergone a *This Morning* makeover and was ready to tackle the Himalayas. I thought of how I must have looked and a picture of Elaine Paige in her mangy cat costume singing 'Memory' came into my head. I simply said, 'Don't ask.' I was too weary to explain.

I felt battered and defeated. I didn't care how I looked, and even the cheerful banter of Big Lynn couldn't reach me. The verdict seemed to matter less and less. Now it seemed to be about honour. Not only were the defendants accusing me of being a liar, but they were also disregarding the abuse at St Anne's by pointing the finger of blame for my situation at my parents instead. They had thrown down the gauntlet. They had attacked those I loved and they were trying to destroy the precious happy memories that I had left.

Very few of us explore our own pasts – for most of us, there is very little reason to. We reach a certain age and we have formed certain opinions, or other people have formed them for us, and we cast people out of our lives based on society's prejudices and values, not because we don't like them.

I remembered the condescending looks Lynn had received on our first day in court. Every suit did a double-take as they spotted the 36 big black stitches on her shaven head, and then looked towards the ground with a knowing nod, as if to say, 'I've seen your sort in A&E on a Friday night. Of course, I was only there because Camilla accidently pushed my head into the consommé.' My oversleeping and turning up late on the second day hadn't helped matters. I was sure they thought Big Lynn and I had been out drinking the night before. We hadn't, of course. We had chatted, we had laughed, and we had lain on our beds talking into the wee small hours, but they had formed their opinion. We were two middle-aged council-estate scallywags who had wandered onto an Eton playing field, and the bullies were closing in on us.

Of course, I had been bitterly disappointed when I had first caught sight of Lynn. She looked as though she had been in a bare-knuckle fight with one of the local tramps and he had hit her over the head with his bottle of Tennent's Super. I had hoped she would have gone for a quieter, more subdued look, something more along the Margaret Thatcher line.

It was impossible to be angry with Big Lynn. She had, after all, made a promise to be with me for the trial, and, bless her, she had stuck to that promise. I was ashamed of myself for thinking as they did. They didn't know Big Lynn as I did. Her enthusiasm for the trial was 100 per cent and then some. At one point she wanted to buy popcorn. She was more than happy to discuss the most minute details pertaining to the days' events, or, come to think of it, anything else our minds wandered off to. 'Get me up there, I'll tell 'em,' she kept saying. Big Lynn would sit rolling cigarettes or plastering cream on her mush. She always had to be doing something, as if she felt guilty just for sitting chatting. I think it was because her family was from the East End.

The last day was a bit of an anticlimax, all told. No one would give any real hints as to which way the case had gone. Fifty–fifty was the best I could get. I sensed my team discussed the real nitty-gritty when I wasn't around. It all seemed to be about case law, not about what had gone on in that courtroom for the previous three days.

I was past caring. I didn't really want to know. I was exhausted. It seemed to me that the whole thing rested on the law's admitted grey area, the statute of limitations. I had researched it on the Internet, looking up cases such as mine and the judgments and the way in which they had superseded each other. I usually fell asleep. If the finest legal minds in the country couldn't work it out, then what chance did I have?

Chapter 30
The Verdict

The judge took almost three weeks to reach his decision regarding my case, and it was an anxious time. Bizarrely, during that tense waiting period, I felt strangely elated: it was as though a huge weight had been lifted from my shoulders. After five years and one and a half days in the witness box, there was nothing more that I could do, except wait.

I had made my statement, and I had been grilled, fried and boiled by the expert psychologists and the learned barristers and the judge. I knew that every word I had spoken was the truth, and I had no criminal record or record of any kind of dishonesty that Omni could have picked up on and used to invalidate my evidence or to 'break' me in the witness box.

Both Big Lynn and I had felt strangely sombre as we packed our cases and headed out onto the mysterious streets of Leeds in search of the coach stop that would take us back to London. We had analysed and dissected all of the points of the trial, and we were both exhausted. But with Lynn it was impossible to stay sombre for very long, and our walking route took us past a Nando's, which was much too tempting to pass. Afterwards, as our coach drove off into the night, I asked Lynn if she had any regrets. 'Yes,' she replied, 'we should have had half a chicken each in Nando's.' And I think she was right.

During this waiting period, I had much time to reflect and ponder as to what had brought me to court, to that temple of justice, and to the position where I trembled every time the telephone rang. Now it all seemed so trivial, even slightly ridiculous. I felt very small and very embarrassed. I wanted to crawl in the corner and hide for causing so much fuss. I felt as though I was starting to parody those crazy women that were supposedly in my head. I had been more than willing to cast myself as the pathetic victim, the nonentity, a bit player in their warped eighteenth-century farce.

The judge knew that I was telling the truth, even though I had no witnesses to support me. I had not been able to contact the people I had wanted to, and those I did have contact with wanted no part of my trial. I didn't blame them for it one bit, and I didn't push it. I honestly believed that the truth would have been enough, and besides, the application to reveal the file of Peter Rands had been successful, and it proved that what I had said was true. However, the laws of this land make it far more complex than that. My case, of course, turned on the limitation point – I waited far too long to bring it to trial, and the argument that I had not wanted to bring the case in my father's lifetime might not be good enough.

In a courtroom, it didn't seem to matter what was right and what was wrong: judges make decisions, and then other judges make decisions after that and overturn them. Barristers and judges spend their entire lifetimes quoting cases at each other and performing the same bizarre courtroom rituals from the time of Dickens. Anyone without a wig hasn't got a clue what is going on. I wasn't sure if that was a good thing or not, and I thanked all the gods there may be that I hadn't decided to study law. I was curious as to whether they would quote my case to the next poor sod they put on the spit.

Taking my case to trial had perhaps been one of the most ridiculous decisions I had ever made in my life; in fact, it was right up there in the top three. It had dominated my life for more than five years. I could say that I had lived, eaten, slept and dreamed of nothing but the eventual day in court, but that would not be true. In fact, I am sure I probably contributed to the continual delays because there were times when I could honestly not bring myself to open my solicitor's letters. I switched off. I carried on living as I always had. I had spent most of my life switching off convent memories by chanting in my head, like Scarlett O'Hara, 'I'll think about that tomorrow.' Mostly that worked, but with the case looming I was forced to confront those memories, even though I just wanted to hide under the duvet and wait there until they went away.

I wondered why I had put myself through the whole ordeal. I had never felt 'damaged', and I had never lived or acted as if I was. I had done the opposite; I felt I had refused to be a victim. I was my own harshest critic. I even wondered if I were trying to use the convent as an excuse for my failures. The psychologists had found plenty to get on with, that was true, but the reality was they had stirred up a nest of crazies that might have been better left alone.

It had been important for the opposing barrister to discredit me on the issue of why it had taken so long for me to bring a claim. 'Why did you not bring the claim sooner?' he had kept repeating. And it was a good point. I had worked as a legal secretary and knew something of the legal system; hence there was no reason why I should not have known it was possible to bring an action. Omni had got me there; I had no real reply. If I said I had not felt damaged, he would have used that to counter with, 'Well, why bring a claim?' They are wizards with semantics, these lawyers.

My real answer would not have been good enough. How could I tell him I would have been way too embarrassed for those I worked with to ever know any of that 'horrible weird stuff' from my past. I already knew it was a relationship killer, so no way was I ever going to reveal any of it outside of the small circle of friends I trusted. Of course, he had managed to make me look more stupid than I had felt.

More importantly, it was the death of my beloved father that led me to dipping a toe into my memories of St Anne's and taking active steps to trace people from the past. It seems I was always making vows, but one that was truly ingrained was not to bring a case during my father's lifetime. He was a compassionate and educated man, and I knew that he was cursed with depression, some of it almost certainly caused by my brother and I spending time in that place, and I had no wish to cause him further pain.

Bringing the claim turned out to be as traumatic and emotional as I had imagined it would be, and worse. But once taken, it is a road from which there is seemingly no turning back. I had made a firm decision from the outset not to pursue or pester any former boarders from St Anne's, because I felt it would be inherently wrong to make people face something they have successfully buried. I have never been one to go along with psychobabble, and mostly think it really is best to let sleeping dogs lie. A courtroom ordeal could tip anyone who is fragile over the edge.

I have never claimed to be one of the 'more seriously injured' claimants, and my claim wasn't huge; it was valued at around £20,000. I had only been at the convent for four or five years; many others had been there much longer and had suffered more serious abuse. In a couple of cases, the former uncles were prosecuted and imprisoned. My case was weakened because I had not been sexually abused, nor had I been approached by detectives or anyone investigating anything from the past. I had made the first move. The fact that I had approached a solicitor worked against me. It raised questions as to my motives.

I had almost half convinced myself that it had been all about the money, that little yellow convertible, that holiday in the sun. But as the case went on, it became a cause. I came across so many sad stories, and I wondered what had happened to those other kids, the ones who had become like brothers and sisters to me. We had shared so much, the dark times and the good, and we had tried to help each other where we could. I wondered if they were OK. I wondered if they had gone on to lead normal, happy lives. I had been devastated to hear of the death of Philip. Handsome, clever, kind: his life should have been so different. If I ever considered giving the whole thing up and abandoning my case, I thought of Philip, and I thought of how £20,000 could have helped him.

The practical side of me tried to imagine what the trial must have cost and how many claims it could have settled. I had indeed been a legal secretary, and I was sure it must have cost several hundred thousand pounds. I wondered how many hundreds of claimants' lives could have been helped by relatively small payouts, which could have been just enough to give recognition to their cause, to validate them. A global apology from the Catholic Church is not enough to salve those wounds inflicted so long ago. We are each unique, we are individuals, we deserve the basic human right to tell our own stories. We want to be heard, we do not want to be brushed away under the carpet, past mistakes that nobody wants to listen to any more. We need the powers that be to acknowledge that the abuse happened and to accept that, for some, it caused enormous emotional scars. They may have had problems with authority, drink or drug abuse, chronic depression, or an inability to form and sustain relationships. Many end up homeless and destitute, and, sadly, many end up dead way too soon.

I had come face to face with adult victims of former care-home abuse, and I had seen how their lives had been devastated by the warped ideology that had been beaten into them as kids. Broken and fragile, they would never be able to speak out. But I could.

I did not know if I was seeking revenge. I know that I had wanted revenge as a child, I had wanted it so badly that I used to cry myself to sleep at night. I never knew how I was going to achieve it, though Mole and I would plan all sorts of scenarios in which we would meet those people again and beat them to a pulp. But as the years went by, those thoughts were largely buried or forgotten.

I did not want to live my life based on hate, and mostly I was able to forget the past. But as I went from one crisis to the next, it would rear its ugly head again and again.

I tried to understand why some nuns or clergy or perverted lay people would behave in the way that they did. I wondered what on earth could have happened to them – maybe they had been victims, too? But their physical attacks were not always spontaneous, motivated by rage or passion: some were premeditated and sustained.

Some attacks were purely for fun. The residue of guilty feelings from my former religion hung over me like a cloud. What was I doing? Why did I want revenge on these people who were old now, and probably frail? It was a moral quandary, one that I tortured myself with as the case dragged on and on. But as more and more details emerged, I found that I was far from the only one to have carried emotional scars from my time at St Anne's; in fact, the abuse I suffered was minor in comparison to many others'.

I was angered to discover that Peter Rands had never been prosecuted, and, worse, the evidence suggests that he continued working with children until the late 1980s. I found that unforgivable and I never forgot the lost life of Philip.

I tried to believe that those people did not behave in that way any more, or at least that they are prevented from behaving that way by law, but life has taught me that wicked people never change.

Peter Rands was alive when my case began. He denied everything, of course, but would not give a sworn statement. Sister Consolata is alive and also denies everything. I hope they are not too reliant on that final absolution.

It was almost three weeks until I received the awaited phone call from my solicitor. I had lost. That was it, the end of the road. I was numb at first, even though I had prepared myself for the worst. I even thought about the ones who had killed themselves at this point. It was not a good result. In fact, it was a disaster. 'If it's any consolation,' my solicitor said, 'I am sure the judge believed you.'

I didn't cry, though, I just lay on my bed and thought, 'Shit.' I couldn't concentrate, not even enough to watch endless reruns of my favourite sitcoms. My head was buzzing with ideas. It was as though a huge, great cloud had been lifted and a whole new world had opened up. I had finally buried my past, it was done and dusted, and I wanted to rub my hands together and say, 'That's it, I've done it. Now I can start living Life Part II.'

I thought about my journey back from Leeds with Big Lynn, our long coach trip and the unavoidable subject: the key events of the trial we had both just endured. Big Lynn had gone straight into clucking mother-hen mode and said losing wasn't possible, I had been brilliant up there. 'And if you do lose, then I shall have something to say about it,' she boomed in her big cockney voice. 'But seriously, though,' she said gently, 'how will you cope?'

I didn't really know how I would feel. I knew losing was a very real possibility, but, strangely, I didn't feel down at the thought. I felt as though it had all been worthwhile: I had got to tell my story, and that was all I ever wanted.

Postscript

Big Lynn died three months after the trial finished. She knew about my book. Losing Big Lynn was devastating. As a family, we still grieve for her, and will do for a long time yet.